THE EXAMINED LIFE

THE
EXAMINED
LIFE

How We Lose and Find Ourselves

Stephen Grosz

Chatto & Windus

LONDON

Published by Chatto & Windus 2013

2 4 6 8 10 9 7 5 3

Copyright © Stephen Grosz 2013

Stephen Grosz has asserted his right under the Copyright, Designs
and Patents Act 1988 to be identified as the author of this work

First published in Great Britain in 2013 by
Chatto & Windus
Random House, 20 Vauxhall Bridge Road,
London SW1V 2SA
www.randomhouse.co.uk

Addresses for companies within The Random House Group Limited can be found at:
www.randomhouse.co.uk/offices.htm

The Random House Group Limited Reg. No. 954009

A CIP catalogue record for this book
is available from the British Library

ISBN 9780701185350

The Random House Group Limited supports The Forest Stewardship Council
(FSC®), the leading international forest certification organisation. Our books
carrying the FSC label are printed on FSC® certified paper. FSC is the only forest
certification scheme endorsed by the leading environmental organisations, including
Greenpeace. Our paper procurement policy can be found at
www.randomhouse.co.uk/environment

Text design © Richard Marston
Typeset in MillerText by Palimpsest Book Production Limited,
Falkirk, Stirlingshire
Printed and bound in Great Britain by
CPI Group (UK) Ltd, Croydon CR0 4YY

To Nicola, Clara and Samuel

We receive and we lose, and we must try to achieve gratitude; and with that gratitude to embrace with whole hearts whatever of life that remains after the losses.

ANDRE DUBUS II, *Broken Vessels*

Contents

Changing

Leaving

Sources and Notes

Acknowledgements

Preface

For the past twenty-five years, I've worked as a psychoanalyst. I've treated patients in psychiatric hospitals, psychotherapy and forensic psychotherapy clinics, child and adolescent units, and private practice. I've seen children, adolescents and adults for consultation, referral and once-a-week psychotherapy. Most of my work, however, has been with adults in psycho-analysis – meeting with one person for fifty minutes, four or five times a week, over a number of years. I have spent more than 50,000 hours with patients. The substance of that work is the substance of this book.

What follows are episodes drawn from day-to-day practice. While I've altered some details in the interest of confidentiality, I've stayed close to the facts: these stories are true.

At one time or another, most of us have felt trapped by things we find ourselves thinking or doing, caught by our own impulses or foolish choices; ensnared in some unhappiness or fear; imprisoned by our own history. We feel unable to go forward and yet we believe that there must be a way. 'I want to change, but not if it means changing,' a patient once said to me in complete innocence. Because my work is about helping people to change, this book is about change. And because change and loss are deeply connected – there cannot be change without loss – loss haunts this book.

The philosopher Simone Weil describes how two prisoners in adjoining cells learn, over a very long period of time, to talk to each other by tapping on the wall. 'The wall is the thing which separates them, but it is also their means of communication,' she writes. 'Every separation is a link.'

This book is about that wall. It's about our desire to talk, to understand and be understood. It's also about listening to each other, not just the words but the gaps in between. What I'm describing here isn't a magical process. It's something that is a part of our everyday lives – we tap, we listen.

Beginnings

How we can be possessed by a story that cannot be told

I want to tell you a story about a patient who shocked me.

When I was first starting out as a psychoanalyst, I rented a small consulting room in Hampstead, on a wide leafy street called Fitzjohns Avenue. It was near a number of well-known psychoanalytic clinics and a few minutes walk from the Freud Museum. At the south end of Fitzjohns Avenue, there is a large bronze statue of Freud.

My consulting room was quiet and spare. There was a desk just large enough for writing up notes and preparing my monthly bills, but no bookshelves or files – the room wasn't for reading or research. As in most consulting rooms, the couch wasn't a couch, but a firm single bed with a dark fitted cover. At the head of the bed was a goose-down cushion, and on top of that a white linen napkin that I changed between patients. The psychoanalyst who rented the room to me had hung one piece of African folk art on the walls many years before. She still used the room in the mornings and I used it in the afternoons. For that reason it was impersonal, ascetic even.

I was working part-time at the Portman Clinic, a forensic outpatient service. In general, patients referred to the Portman had broken the law; some had committed violent or sexual crimes. I saw patients of all ages and I wrote quite a few court reports. At the same time, I was building up my private practice. My plan was to reserve my mornings for clinic work; in the afternoons I hoped to see private patients who had less extreme or pressing problems.

As it turned out, my first private patients were fairly demanding too. Looking back, I see many reasons why these first cases were difficult. Partly, there was my own inexperience. I think it takes time – it took me time – to realise just how very different people are from each other. And it probably didn't help that I'd received a number of referrals from senior psychiatrists and psychoanalysts trying to help me get started. Doctors often refer patients to junior analysts that they don't want to see themselves or can't place anywhere else. And so I was struggling with:

Miss A., a twenty-year-old undergraduate. Although the psychoanalyst who'd assessed her described Miss A. as 'suffering uncontrollable bouts of crying, depression and pervasive feelings of inadequacy', she presented as a cheerful young woman who insisted that she did not need treatment.

In time, however, I learned that she was bulimic and regularly, compulsively, cut herself. Because she had only attended her sessions sporadically, two other therapists had given up seeing her.

Professor B., a forty-year-old research scientist, married with two children. He'd recently been accused of plagiarising a rival's work. The vice chancellor had referred the matter to the disciplinary committee. If he was found guilty – and Professor B. told me it was likely that he would be – he might be given the chance to resign discreetly. His physician had put him on antidepressants and asked me to see him for psycho-analysis. Professor B. vacillated wildly between states of hectic triumph – mocking colleagues on the disciplinary committee, for example – and utter dejection.

Mrs C., who owned and operated a small restaurant with her husband; she was a mother of three. She wanted help because she felt anxious and suffered panic attacks. In our first meeting she said that she 'found it difficult to relate honestly', but it was only after several months of therapy that she told me that she was having an affair with her children's nanny, a woman who had been working for the family for the past seven years, since shortly after the birth of her first child. Now – contrary to an agreement with her husband – Mrs C. was secretly trying to get pregnant because she could not bear the thought of losing her nanny.

Another of my earliest patients was a young man named

Peter. He was undergoing treatment at a large psychiatric hospital nearby. Three months before we met, Peter hid in the cupboard of a local church, where he tried to kill himself by taking an overdose of various drugs and then slitting his wrists. He also stabbed himself in the neck, chest and arms with a small knife. He was discovered by a cleaner. Although she was frightened, the cleaner held him as they waited for the ambulance. 'Who did this?' she asked him. 'Tell me, who did this to you?'

The consultant psychiatrist at the hospital asked me if I'd see Peter five times a week for psychoanalysis. She felt that daily therapy, together with a weekly meeting with her, was Peter's best chance for recovery, for returning home to his fiancée and to his work.

Peter was twenty-seven and worked as a structural engineer. Before he was hospitalised, he and his fiancée had bought a one-bedroom flat outside London. He had been having difficulties at work and was anxious about money – but none of this seemed to explain his violent attack on himself. Part of my job, then, was to work with Peter to identify the causes of his suicide attempt – if we couldn't understand the forces that had pushed him to attack himself, there was every reason to think it would happen again.

Peter was tall and lanky, but carried himself as some depressed people do, shoulders hunched forward, head down. His manner was depressed too – he spoke haltingly, with little eye contact. Once positioned on the couch, he hardly ever moved.

Peter attended all of his sessions, and was almost never late. After several months, he left hospital and was able to return to his life. But increasingly, in our sessions, I felt him disappear to a place I couldn't find, let alone understand. 'You've been silent a long time – can you tell me what you've been thinking about?' I asked in one session.

'A holiday in Devon – when I was a child,' he replied.

There was a long pause. Could he tell me more? He replied that he wasn't thinking about anything in particular, he was just thinking about being alone.

I had the thought that he wanted to be away from me, on holiday from analysis, and told him so. 'Could be,' he replied.

It was as if Peter was trying to protect himself from my intrusiveness, as if he was complying with the conventions of analysis – being on time and answering my questions, for example – but in such a way as to prevent any meaningful connection developing between us. He seemed to have little faith in our talking.

But I did learn that Peter had a history of making friends and then turning on them. In his professional life too he'd quietly go about his work, then suddenly get into a row with his boss and quit. This had happened several times. I tried to use this information to show Peter that he seemed to have two psychological positions open to him – acquiescence or blowing everything up. He seemed to agree, but I never felt this idea was meaningful to him. And soon this pattern was enacted in the analysis. Peter went from going along with me to mocking me. After one particularly tumultuous week, Peter stopped coming to his sessions. I wrote to him, proposing that he talk to me about his decision to end his treatment, but I received no reply.

I contacted the psychiatrist, who told me that Peter had stopped seeing her too.

Two months later, a letter arrived from Peter's fiancée, informing me that he had taken his own life. She explained that, during the month leading up to his death, Peter had grown increasingly disturbed and withdrawn. The family had held a funeral at West London Crematorium the week before. She wrote that she was grateful for my attempts to help him. I sent a letter of condolence to her, and then informed Peter's psychiatrist.

I'd known that Peter was a high-risk patient. When I took him on, I'd enlisted the help of a supervisor, an experienced psychoanalyst who'd written a book on suicide. He had repeatedly pointed out to me the many ways in which Peter seemed to idealise death. Now I went to see him again, anxious that there was something I'd missed. My supervisor tried to reassure me. 'Who knows?' he said. 'Being in analysis with you might have *kept* him from suicide for the past year.' Still, Peter's death disturbed me greatly. Of course, I knew that we all have the capacity to act in self-destructive ways, nevertheless I had a kind of faith that the desire to live was more powerful. Now, instead, I felt its fragility. Peter's suicide made me feel that the battle between the forces of life and death was far more evenly pitched.

Six months later, I received a message on my answering machine. I heard the unmistakable sounds of a public telephone – the pips, the coins falling – and then Peter's voice: 'It's me. I'm not dead. I was wondering if I could come and talk to you. I'm at my old number.'

The instant I heard Peter's voice, I felt faint, confused. For a moment I persuaded myself that the answering machine was malfunctioning, that I was listening to a very old message from Peter that had never been erased. And then I laughed – out of anger, out of relief. And because I was stunned.

That evening, when I wrote to the consultant psychiatrist to tell her that Peter wasn't dead, I did what many people do when they're angry: I made a joke. 'Unless there are payphones in hell,' I wrote, 'Peter is still alive. He left a message on my answering machine earlier today, asking for an appointment.'

Peter came to see me the following week. In a matter-of-fact way, he told me that he, not his fiancée, had written to inform me of his death. He'd also intercepted my condolence note. 'It was touching,' he said.

'Oh that *is* interesting,' my supervisor said. 'It's surprising this doesn't happen more often. When you think of all those adolescents who say "you'll be sorry when I kill myself" – you'd think more of them would fake it.' We decided that I should only take Peter on again if I felt he was really prepared to make a serious commitment.

After several meetings, Peter and I agreed to resume his sessions. Ultimately, his disappearance and return proved helpful, because it clarified something that we had never understood: his need to shock others.

In the sessions that followed it slowly became clear that Peter enjoyed thinking about the distress he caused when he suddenly quit work or ended a friendship. He'd blown up the analysis twice – first when he quit and then, a second time, when he faked his suicide. In the first phase of his analysis, I hadn't realised just how attached Peter was to violently upsetting others. But why?

Peter's parents had divorced when he was two and his mother had remarried soon after. During this second phase of his analysis, Peter sought out his biological father and spoke frankly with his mother. He discovered that his mother had been having an affair with the man who became his stepfather, and that his father and mother both drank heavily. He also discovered that the first two years of his life were very different from the story he'd been told. His mother and father both admitted that they couldn't cope and had been violent with him when he was a baby.

Peter told me that his dad didn't remember much, just that it was a terrible, unhappy time, an unhappy marriage. 'My mother cried, she kept saying that she was sorry,' Peter said. 'She was only twenty when I was born and no one was there to help her. She said that sometimes she felt she was just going crazy.'

Her confession gave Peter some relief. For as long as he could remember, he had felt afraid. He told me that it helped to know that he was frightened of *something*. For a small child, violence is an overwhelming, uncontrollable and terrifying experience – and its emotional effects can endure for a lifetime. The trauma becomes internalised, it's what takes hold of us in the absence of another's empathy. So why did Peter turn on those close to him?

Peter's behaviour made it clear that he couldn't allow himself to feel weak. Dependence for him was dangerous. Peter's story might be summed up as, 'I'm the attacker who traumatises, never the baby who is hurt.' But Peter also felt bound to turn on himself. When Peter assaulted himself in the church, he enacted this same story. As he told me, 'I thought – you pathetic little crybaby. I can do this to you and you can't stop me.'

I believe that all of us try to make sense of our lives by telling our stories, but Peter was possessed by a story that he couldn't tell. Not having the words, he expressed himself by other means. Over time I learned that Peter's behaviour was the language he used to speak to me. Peter told his story by making me feel what it was like to be him, of the anger, confusion and shock that he must have felt as a child.

The author Karen Blixen said, 'All sorrows can be borne if you put them into a story or tell a story about them.' But what if a person can't tell a story about his sorrows? What if his story tells him?

Experience has taught me that our childhoods leave in us stories like this – stories we never found a way to voice, because no one helped us to find the words. When we cannot find a way of telling our story, our story tells us – we dream these stories, we develop symptoms, or we find ourselves acting in ways we don't understand.

Two years after Peter left his message on my answering machine, we agreed to stop his psychoanalysis. I thought there was more work to do, but he felt that it was time.

All of this happened many years ago. Since then Peter hasn't asked to meet again, but I did run into him recently, at the cinema. We recognised each other across the lobby. Peter said something to the woman he was standing with and they walked over. He extended his hand and then he introduced me to his wife.

On laughter

Monday, the first day after the Easter break – it was warm, bright. I opened the windows in my consulting room a little and then went out to get my last patient of the morning. Lily stood up as soon as she heard me. 'It's such a relief to be back here,' she said. 'I had a crazy time at home.'

Lily had just returned from a trip to New York to visit her parents with her nine-month-old daughter, Alice. The flight from London had been terrible. After navigating her way through the New York airport with Alice and all of their belongings, she found her mother standing outside on the sidewalk. 'She hugged me the way she always does,' Lily said. 'She closes her eyes and pats my back – as if I have fleas.'

Her mother opened the car door and Monty, her slobbering fifty-pound golden retriever, jumped out. 'He pushes his nose into my jeans, which is sort of embarrassing. And I'm wondering why she's brought a dog to the airport – it's not like they have a station wagon. My mom says, "I thought this would be a good way to introduce them to each other." So Alice is in her car seat in the back, I'm next to her, and Monty is up front, riding shotgun.'

Throughout the visit, neither of Lily's parents showed much interest in her life. They left their two televisions blaring and ate their meals crammed around the kitchen counter. Her father often ate with his laptop propped open next to his plate.

'On my last night, after three glasses of wine, I tell my parents that when I get back to London I'm going to send them a thousand photos of Alice. You have to understand, there are photos in every room of the house. There's a whole flotilla of photos on the grand piano, but nowhere is there a single photo of their first grandchild.

'And my mom says, "Oh my gosh, didn't you see it? It's my favourite!" And she goes into the bedroom, rummages around in the dresser, and pulls out a picture of Alice. She smiles and says, "Aww, I love that picture." Then my dad says, "Aww, I love that picture." And then I say, "Aww, I love it too." But I'm thinking: what the fuck? Does she think I have X-ray eyes?'

I stifled a laugh.

Lily was quiet for a moment. 'My last night there I had a strange dream. It was a nightmare actually. What happened was upsetting, but I didn't feel upset.'

In the dream, Lily was in a group of people standing by a lake. She watched a small girl swim out to a wooden raft – the girl struggled but was able to make it and to pull herself up.

There was a flash of lightning and a clap of thunder. The girl was in danger, but no one was concerned – where was the little girl's mother, her father? Lily asked her parents to watch Alice and she swam out to the girl. The lake was black and choppy; it was a struggle to keep the girl's head above water. When they got back on to the shore, Lily lifted the girl out of the water, and then saw that her parents were standing there alone – Alice was nowhere to be seen.

Lily was sure that the last bit – *Alice was nowhere to be seen* – must have been about the tucked-away photograph. But what about the rest of it?

'Does the dream remind you of anything?' I asked.

It reminded her of the lake near her old boarding school. Every autumn, one or two of the new students were tossed in the lake by some of the older boys. The boys tended to pick the cockiest boys and the prettiest girls. Those first weeks at boarding school – when she was so homesick – she was kind of pleased to be chosen.

In the weeks that followed, some of the older girls in her dorm sought her out. They teased her about sex and tried to persuade her to visit one of the senior boys in his room. Lily was fourteen and had never kissed a boy.

One evening, after dinner, a senior girl took her into the toilets and taught her how to make herself sick by sticking her fingers down her throat. 'It's like giving head, just open up and take it in,' the girl told her.

Boarding school got more and more overwhelming. Lily consoled herself with the thought that she was bright and would do well, that in the next year or two she'd get a boy-friend, fall in love – everything would work out. But it wasn't happening like that. Lily had trouble eating and sleeping. She never missed a class, but she felt increasingly frantic. 'I didn't get depressed; I just went faster and faster. The wheels started to come off the bus – I couldn't keep my head above water.'

'So the girl in the dream is you,' I said.

'But if that's me, how can I look after Alice?'

'That may be what the dream is about.'

Lily admitted that she *had* found it difficult to stay focused on Alice when she was with her parents. During her stay she'd regressed – she'd felt less and less like her grown-up self, less and less like the mother she was. 'It was like, you know, where the kidnap victim forgets the outside world and starts to think like their captor? Stockholm syndrome.'

It occurred me that Lily was reworking her visit home into a series of comic bits. At every turn in the narrative, just when I expected her to tell me that she'd felt hurt or upset, I got a punchline – 'as if I have fleas'; 'does she think I have X-ray eyes?'

From the pavement outside, through the open window, came the sound of children shouting and giggling on their way to a nearby playground. As Lily and I waited for the children to pass, I found myself thinking about the word punchline – its violence is so out in the open. Was it from Punch and Judy?

A few months earlier, just before Christmas, one of the local shops had hired a Punch and Judy puppet show. My children and I stood and watched the show: Judy went out, leaving Mr Punch at home to look after the baby. As always, the chaotic Mr Punch forgot about the baby, sat on the baby, even eventually bit the baby. Judy returned, the stick was fetched and the knockabout began. I was freezing and wanted to go home; my children were captivated. We stayed till the end.

'One of the problems with your joking is that we can feel as if we've talked about something that troubles you – your arrival at the airport, Alice's photo being kept in the dresser – and we *have* talked about it, but it hasn't really been dealt with,' I said.

'If I didn't laugh about their stuff, I'd be angry most of the time.'

'Your jokes are aggressive, you get your revenge, and you feel a bit better. Your humour seems to work: you don't hurt so much afterwards. But you also seem to lose the drive to better understand the situation.'

'My jokes defuse my anger, but they defuse it to the point that I just accept my parents' behaviour. I stop thinking about it.'

'Exactly,' I said.

Lily paused and then said she wasn't so sure. She *did* think about the situation with her parents – it *was* a nightmare. But there wasn't anything that could be done.

The word nightmare reminded me of her dream. I told her I was struck by the thing she'd said just before describing it – 'it was a nightmare, what happened was upsetting, but I didn't feel upset.'

I said, 'The aim of the dream might have been to reassure yourself that you can be in a nightmare and yet not feel it. Not just keep your head above water, but numb yourself to your parents' lack of concern.'

'Can you imagine what would happen if I *didn't* numb myself?' she asked. 'If my parents knew what I thought, it'd be the end of what remains of our relationship. I don't have the skill to discuss with them the things that bother me. It'd all go wrong. My mom would deny that she was doing anything aggressive – she'd say, "It's just a photo, honey."' Her voice trailed off. 'It works, Mr Grosz – it works.'

Early in her psychoanalysis, I'd noticed that Lily's voice went up at the end of sentences, even when she wasn't asking a question. This inflection put pressure on me to speak. At the time, we figured out that this was because my silences made her uneasy. She wanted me to speak, so as to hear in my voice if I agreed with her or not.

I told Lily that I thought she might want me to laugh for similar reasons. My laughter meant that we were in agreement – that we were the good guys, and her parents the bad guys. My laughter absolved her of guilt – she didn't have to feel bad about making fun of her parents.

She told me it *was* a relief when I laughed, and then she was silent. Neither of us spoke for some time. I began to assume that Lily had looked at her wristwatch and decided, as there were only a few moments left, to stop for the day. I felt she'd left the room.

And then she said, 'I was remembering my breakdown at boarding school, the experience of calling home in the middle of the night from a payphone behind the dorm, the bugs buzzing around the fluorescent light. I was crying hysterically, "Please can I come home, please can I come home?" and being told, "No, you can't come home." Then, as things got worse and worse and worse, I forced myself to stay. But something had changed in me. My breakdown was like a furnace and what was burned away was any belief in my own feelings.'

As I listened to her memory, I also heard her dream, *the girl was in danger, but no one was concerned – where was the little girl's mother, her father?*

She went on, 'Even now it's very hard for me to trust my feelings. But when you laugh it means you believe my feelings, my reality. When you laugh, I know that you see things exactly the way I do – that you wouldn't have said no, you'd have let me come home.'

How praise can cause a loss of confidence

Rounding the corner into the nursery school classroom to collect my daughter, I overheard the nursery assistant tell her, 'You've drawn the most beautiful tree. Well done.' A few days later, she pointed to another of my daughter's drawings and remarked, 'Wow, you really are an artist!'

On both occasions, I found myself at a loss. How could I explain to the nursery assistant that I would prefer it if she didn't praise my daughter?

Nowadays, we lavish praise on our children. Praise, self-confidence and academic performance, it is commonly believed, rise and fall together. But current research suggests otherwise – over the past decade, a number of studies on self-esteem have come to the conclusion that praising a child as 'clever' may not help her at school. In fact, it might cause her to under-perform. Often a child will react to praise by quitting – why make a new drawing if you have already made 'the best'? Or a child may simply repeat the same work – why draw something new, or in a new way, if the old way always gets applause?

In a now famous 1998 study of children aged ten and eleven, psychologists Carol Dweck and Claudia Mueller asked 128 children to solve a series of mathematical problems. After completing the first set of simple exercises, the researchers gave each child just one sentence of praise. Some were praised for their intellect – 'You did really well, you're so clever'; others for their hard work – 'You did really well, you must have tried really hard.' Then the researchers had the children try a more challenging set of problems. The results were dramatic. The students who were praised for their effort showed a greater willingness to work out new approaches. They also showed more resilience and tended to attribute their failures to insufficient effort, not to a lack of intelligence. The children who had been praised for their cleverness worried more about failure, tended to choose tasks that confirmed what they already knew, and displayed less tenacity when the problems got harder. Ultimately, the thrill created by being told 'You're so clever' gave way to an increase in anxiety and a drop in self-esteem, motivation and perform-ance. When asked by the researchers to write to children in another school, recounting their experience, some of the 'clever' children lied, inflating their scores. In short, all it took to knock these youngsters' confidence, to make them so unhappy that they lied, was one sentence of praise.

Why are we so committed to praising our children?

In part, we do it to demonstrate that we're different from our parents. In *Making Babies*, a memoir about becoming a mother, Anne Enright observes, 'In the old days – as we call the 1970s, in Ireland – a mother would dispraise her child automatically . . . "She's a monkey," a mother might say, or "Street angel, home devil," or even my favourite, "She'll have me in an early grave." It was all part of growing up in a country where praise of any sort was taboo.' Of course, this wasn't the case in Ireland alone. Recently, a middle-aged Londoner told me, 'My mum called me things I'd never call my kids – too clever by half, cheeky, precocious and show-off. Forty years on, I want to shout at my mum, "What's so terrible about showing off?"'

Now, wherever there are small children – at the local playground, at Starbucks and at nursery school – you will hear the background music of praise: 'Good boy,' 'Good girl,' 'You're the best.' Admiring our children may temporarily lift our self-esteem by signalling to those around us what fantastic parents we are and what terrific kids we have – but it isn't doing much for a child's sense of self. In trying so hard to be different from our parents, we're actually doing much the same thing – doling out empty praise the way an earlier generation doled out thoughtless criticism. If we do it to avoid thinking about our child and her world, and about what our child feels, then praise, just like criticism, is ultimately expressing our indifference.

Which brings me back to the original problem – if praise doesn't build a child's confidence, what does?

Shortly after qualifying as a psychoanalyst, I discussed all this with an eighty-year-old woman named Charlotte Stiglitz. Charlotte – the mother of the Nobel Prize-winning economist Joseph Stiglitz – taught remedial reading in northwestern Indiana for many years. 'I don't praise a small child for doing what they ought to be able to do,' she told me. 'I praise them when they do something really difficult – like sharing a toy or showing patience. I also think it is important to say "thank you". When I'm slow in getting a snack for a child, or slow to help them and they have been patient, I thank them. But I wouldn't praise a child who is playing or reading.' No great rewards, no terrible punishments – Charlotte's focus was on what a child did and how that child did it.

I once watched Charlotte with a four-year-old boy, who was drawing. When he stopped and looked up at her – perhaps expecting praise – she smiled and said, 'There is a lot of blue in your picture.' He replied, 'It's the pond near my grand-mother's house – there is a bridge.' He picked up a brown crayon, and said, 'I'll show you.' Unhurried, she talked to the child, but more importantly she observed, she listened. She was present.

Being present builds a child's confidence because it lets the child know that she is worth thinking about. Without this, a child might come to believe that her activity is just a means to gain praise, rather than an end in itself. How can we expect a child to be attentive, if we've not been attentive to her?

Being present, whether with children, with friends, or even with oneself, is always hard work. But isn't this attentiveness – the feeling that someone is trying to think about us – something we want more than praise?

The gift of pain

Mr N. rang me one day in early June because several weeks earlier his twenty-one-year-old son, Matt, had pointed an unloaded starter's pistol at a police officer who was trying to arrest him for disorderly conduct. Matt was now out on bail for a serious firearms offence and he was continuing to act recklessly. In violation of the conditions of his bail, he was staying out late drinking with friends, sometimes not coming home for days. He was getting into fights. His parents, who both worked as teachers, were beginning to accept the fact that Matt would probably go to prison.

Matt's parents had adopted him when he was two years old. Matt's father told me what he knew of Matt's early life: shortly after his birth, Matt and his seventeen-year-old birth mother had left her parents' home, moving first to an emergency shelter and then from place to place. His birth mother, a drug user, was incapable of caring for a baby. Malnourished and ill, Matt was taken into care when he was a year old. He had spent time in several different foster homes before being adopted by Mr N. and his wife. From early on, he had proven to be a difficult and uncompromising child, and, as a result, his parents had decided not to adopt again.

Several days later, Matt came to see me for a consultation. He flopped into a chair facing me, and began to talk quite openly about some of the problems he faced. He told me about two men, brothers, who lived in his neighbourhood and were out to get him – these men were dangerous and had stabbed someone he knew. Matt's situation was alarming but, as he talked, I began to notice that I didn't feel particularly alarmed. Nothing seemed to be missing from his words; his speech was energetic and clear. But I found it difficult to get involved in his story. I was easily distracted by the sounds of cars outside my consulting room and caught myself thinking about some errands I wanted to run at lunchtime. In fact, every attempt I made to think about Matt's story, to take note of his words, was like trying to run uphill in a dream.

This sort of gap between what a person says and what he makes you feel is not uncommon – think of the friend who rings you when you're down, talks to you in an encouraging, supportive way, but leaves you feeling worse. The space between Matt's words and the feelings he provoked in me was enormous. He was describing a life that was frightening, but

I didn't feel frightened for him. I felt uncharacteristically disengaged.

In trying to comprehend my indifference to Matt and his situation, I imagined a series of scenes from his earliest months. I saw a small baby crying – I'm hungry, feed me; I'm wet, change me; I'm frightened, hold me – and being ignored by an unresponsive mother. I had the idea that one consequence of Matt's early experiences could be that he did not know how to make someone feel concern for him, because he did not learn this from his mother. He seemed never to have acquired a skill that we all need: the ability to make another person worry about us.

And what did Matt feel? He too seemed indifferent to his own situation. When I asked him what he felt about his arrest by the police he replied, 'I'm cool. Why?' I tried again. 'You don't seem to be very anxious for yourself,' I said. 'You could have been shot.' He shrugged.

I began to realise that Matt did not register his own emotions. In the course of our two-hour conversation, he seemed either to pick up and employ my descriptions of his feelings or to infer his emotions from the behaviour of others. For example, he said he didn't know why he had pointed the gun at the police officer. I suggested he might have been angry. 'Yeah, I was angry,' Matt replied. 'What did you feel when you were angry?' I asked. 'You know, the police, they were very angry with me. My parents were very angry with me. Everyone was very angry with me,' he replied. 'But what did you feel?' I asked. 'They were all really shouting at me,' he told me.

Typically, what brings a potential patient to a consultation is the pressure of his immediate suffering. In this case it was Matt's father, not Matt, who had telephoned for an appointment. Matt had learned at an early age to deaden his feelings and to distrust those who offered him help. Our encounter was no different. Matt did not feel enough emotional pain to overcome his suspicions and accept my offer to meet again.

In 1946, while working in a leprosy sanatorium, the physician Paul Brand discovered that the deformities of leprosy were not an intrinsic part of the disease, but rather a consequence of the progressive devastation of infection and injury, which occurred because the patient was unable to feel pain. In 1972, he wrote: 'If I had one gift which I could give to people with leprosy, it would be the gift of pain.' Matt suffered from a kind of psychological leprosy; unable to feel his emotional pain, he was forever in danger of permanently, maybe fatally, damaging himself.

After Matt left my office and before writing up my notes, I did what I sometimes do after a knotty, affecting consultation. I walked round the corner to buy a takeaway coffee and then returned to my consulting room to zone out by reading who knows what on the Internet. The truth of the matter is this:

there is a bit of Matt in each of us. At one time or another, we all try to silence painful emotions. But when we succeed in feeling nothing we lose the only means we have of knowing what hurts us, and why.

A safe house

'Hold on,' he says, 'I forgot to put the do-not-disturb notice on the door.'

I hear my patient put the receiver down, cross the room, open and close a door. I hear the muffled sound of him walking back and I imagine his hotel room. I calculate the time – it is 5.45 p.m. in Brussels.

He picks up the receiver. 'I'm so sorry. I should've done that before I rang you. I was thinking about something.'

I hear him take a sip of tea or coffee, and replace a cup in its saucer.

'Do you know what a safe house is?' he asks. He tells me that he'd watched a segment on the BBC about Americans who are building safe rooms or deluxe safe houses. 'You can imagine the snide, anti-American tone of the segment: "look at what those kooky Americans are spending their money on now". But the effect on me was precisely the opposite of what the producers intended. I was moved.'

One scene in particular struck him – a father and his teenage son, sitting on the floor of the father's bedroom. The father shows his son some of the things he keeps in a cardboard box under the bed – a water purification kit, a multi-band self-powered radio, a reel of fishing line. He tells his son that after the apocalypse there won't be any supermarkets where you can buy fish.

My patient feels close to this man. The father is spending all of his savings trying to protect his family. He just wants to feel safe. 'It's mad, he's mad – but I understand it.' He tells me he's worried that he is like that father, always preparing for some calamity.

I hear him take another sip. 'I'm just as crazy, always thinking about my house in France,' he says. 'I've never told you about it.'

The first thing he wants me to know about his house is that it isn't grand. It's not some imposing chateau – it's a farmhouse really, surrounded by fields and forests. It has about it that deep silence you find in the woods in Scotland – the very opposite of London. There's no noise, no disturbance. He doesn't have to see his neighbours' big banker houses.

In fact, several weeks before, he received a letter from the council about his London neighbours' request for permission to develop their already vulgar, overblown town house. He couldn't think about it – he was that angry. Of course, he should have written to the council to object to the development, 'but I couldn't. My wife had to do it. I thought about the house in France – that calmed me.'

And there are times – like just a few minutes ago – when his wife leaves the hotel room, before it's time for his session to begin, moments when he is alone, when he will imagine himself in the house in France. 'It's not time to ring yet, there's a space, a gap, and the next thing I know, I'm gone – lost in my mad architecture.'

I ask him what he means by 'mad'.

He says that what makes it mad is his incessant tweaking, his reconfiguring. He thinks about redecorating, remodelling – adding rooms, doors, windows. 'What would the view be like if I change the shape of this room, turn the house on its foundation, or move it to the top of a neighbouring hill? I do a lot of that sort of thinking, and then there's the bargaining.'

He tells me that it is very difficult for him to talk about all this – much harder than talking about his depression, or his panic attacks. He's not surprised he's telling me about it during a telephone session – it is easier this way, less embarrassing.

This evening, for example, after his wife, Anna, had left and while he was waiting for the start of our session, he had imagined trading everything he has to make the house just right. He would give up his home in London and all of his possessions, probably his position in the government too, but what he would get in return was this: an income of £500 per week and, also, the house exactly as he'd like it to be.

The aim of these negotiations isn't to get something luxurious, quite the opposite – friends would wonder why he had downsized to this plain house in the deserted French countryside. Why had he given up so much comfort? 'We'd become inconspicuous, modest – utterly unenviable.'

I hear him take another sip.

'It's my safe house,' he says. If he's stuck in some pointless meeting, or some crappy hotel by himself – or he's in London and Anna pops out to the shops – he imagines himself in his house in France, or he thinks about some possible alterations.

I tell him that feeling cut off, or separated from Anna, seems to make him feel anxious and angry – separation unsettles him. He may think about his house in France in order to recover his equilibrium.

I hear him take a sip and return the cup to its saucer. 'I thought you were going to say that I think about my house in France when I find reality intolerable. But yes,' he tells me, 'separation *does* disturb me.'

After Oxford, he says, but before going to Harvard, he and

Anna spent the summer in Italy. Up until then, he'd only been to Paris a couple of times. Travelling about from town to town made him anxious; he couldn't shake off the uncomfortable feeling that somehow he would lose Anna, that he would turn around and she'd be gone. Every morning, before leaving their *pensione*, he'd make her promise that should they become separated, she would immediately make her way to the city centre, to the steps of the cathedral. That was their meeting place. 'Whenever I imagine the house in France, I picture Anna in the sitting room, waiting for me – it's like the cathedral, our meeting place.'

I hear him moving around the room. 'Don't worry Mr Grosz, I'm pouring out some more tea, I'm not in the bathroom.'

Some days, he tells me, he is continually thinking about the house: visualising a different colour of paint in this room, a larger doorway in that room. He sketches floor plans, views of the interior. Today, during a meeting, he sketched a view of the hallway, from the front door towards the kitchen. If I were to ask him what's in the larder he could tell me every item on every shelf. But mostly he thinks about the rooms, their reconstruction, their proportions. It's ridiculous, he says, he knows this house better than his home in London.

It must be an escape from the real world, he tells me. The house in France must be connected to some make-believe place he invented as a child. He despised his parents' drunken rows, his mother's tantrums, her violent temper. 'I was always in a book, or a daydream, trying to get away from the noise of their fights. You'll probably say I was trying to get away from the noise of their fights *and* my hatred of them – and that would be true.'

He tells me he's embarrassed, ashamed that he can't sit in a hotel room for a few minutes on his own like a normal person. I don't understand it, he says. 'I worry that my architecture undermines my sense of reality.'

'Maybe,' I say. 'But it could be that your architecture helps you to preserve your sense of reality. You're not thinking about your house in France all of the time. It seems to be something you do when you're cut off, frightened or angry.'

'That's a very charitable reading of what I'm trying to describe, but I'm not sure. It doesn't explain my incessant redecorating, or my bizarre haggling – the "I'll give up everything if only I can have" . . . whatever.'

No, I say, it doesn't explain his bartering. 'That seems more like the sort of thing a frightened child might do.'

I hear him move again, perhaps stand up.

He tells me that there's a story by Joyce, he thinks it's in *Dubliners*. He read it during his first year at university, but he hasn't looked at it since then – the ending was upsetting, too disturbing. At the end of the story, the father – who has been drinking – returns home and discovers that his wife is at church and his son has let the fire go out. The father's going to have to wait for his dinner and the little boy tries to calm him down. He tells his father he'll make him his dinner, but the father won't be appeased. He gets a walking stick, rolls up his sleeves, and then starts to beat the little boy. There is no escape. The drunk father keeps hitting the little boy over and over again. There is blood. The little boy is begging and then the begging turns to bargaining – 'Don't beat me Pa, don't beat me and I'll say a Hail Mary for you. I'll say a Hail Mary for you Pa, if you don't beat me.'

That's how it felt when his mother slapped and punched him – 'Don't hit me Mummy, I'll be good, I'll be a good boy Mummy.' And when that didn't work, he tells me, 'I begged God – "Stop her beating me God, stop her beating me. I'll be good. I'll give you anything, everything, if you just make me safe. Please God, please."'

I hear him breathing. I have the sense he is trying not to cry. He says, 'Mr Grosz?'

'Yes?'

'My house has a magic door.'

'A magic door?'

A year earlier, he'd been on a long-haul flight that had a stopover in Hong Kong. An hour after leaving Hong Kong there was a bang, then the sound of wind rushing through the cabin. The oxygen masks released. The plane dropped rapidly from 30,000 feet. He believed he was about to die. 'I thought that if I could just get up and open the cockpit door, I'd step into my house. I could be home, safe. I was about to take off the oxygen mask and undo my seat belt when the plane levelled out.'

A stalled Underground train, a traffic jam – he can get up and walk through the door, into his house. A lot of his thinking is about the magic door – what does he have to give up to have it? 'It's crazy,' he says, 'isn't it?'

I tell him that I don't think it's crazy. A little boy who is being punched would give anything for a magic door.

'I don't think much about my childhood. When I do, I don't remember a great deal. It all seems so long ago, dead. I think to myself that *was* my childhood – not, that *is* my childhood. It's not alive in me.'

Neither of us speaks. After a minute or so I suddenly worry that we might have been cut off.

'I'm still here,' he says. He is silent for a moment. 'According to my watch our time's almost up. I don't want to say any more now. Tomorrow I have a drinks party that I have to attend, so I'll have to stop fifteen minutes early, I'm very sorry.'

'Thank you for letting me know.'

'Mr Grosz?'

'Yes?'

'I don't really have a house in France. You do know that, don't you?'

Telling Lies

On secrets

His doctor's letter described him as a pathological liar – could I offer an assessment, maybe see him for psychotherapy?

Philip came to see me for an interview one April, some years ago now. His doctor had decided to refer him after bumping into Philip's wife at a local bookshop. She'd taken his hand, holding back tears. Would it be a good idea, she'd wondered, for them to discuss the remaining treatment options for Philip's lung cancer?

During his first meeting with me, Philip (who was perfectly healthy, as his GP had told me) listed some of the lies he'd recently told. At a school fund-raiser, he'd told his daughter's music teacher that he was the son of a famous composer – a man who was widely known to be unmarried and gay. Just before that, he'd told his father-in-law, a sports journalist, that he'd once been selected as a reserve for the UK men's archery team. The first lie he could remember telling was to a classmate.

When Philip was eleven or twelve, he'd insisted that he'd been recruited by MI5 to train as an agent. He described his headmaster's admonishment: 'For goodness' sake – if you're going to lie, at least do a better job of it.'

The headmaster was right, Philip was a dreadful liar. While each lie seemed tailored to wow the listener, they were also pointlessly excessive – wildly risky. 'You don't seem to worry about people thinking you're a liar,' I told him.

He shrugged.

He told me that his listeners rarely challenged him. His wife did not confront him about his miraculous recovery, just as she had seemed to accept the news of his cancer. Others, like his father-in-law, were almost certainly more sceptical, but also remained silent. When I asked him about the effect his lying had on his career – he worked as a television producer – he told me that everyone in the industry lied: 'It's part of the skill set.'

As far as I could tell, Philip didn't empathise with the people to whom he had lied – for the most part, he just didn't seem to care. That is, until the week before he came to see me. His seven-year-old daughter had asked for his help with her French homework; he'd always told her that he was fluent. Now, instead of admitting that he didn't speak French, he told her that he just couldn't remember the names of the farm animals in her exercise book. She became silent and looked away – he saw her realise that he had lied to her.

Throughout the consultation I was struck by Philip's frankness. But I knew that if he was to be himself with me – if he was to bring all of himself into our work – he would, at some point, lie to me. It happened soon enough. A month into treatment, he stopped paying his bill. He told me that he'd misplaced his chequebook, but that he would settle his account as soon as he found it. The next month he told me that he had donated his month's salary to the Freud Museum.

After five months of tall tales, I had to inform him that we would stop at the end of that month unless he settled his debt. Just as he was about to leave what was to have been our final session, he took a cheque from his pocket and handed it to me.

I was relieved to be paid but uncertain about what had happened between us. Philip had told increasingly blatant lies and I'd become increasingly withdrawn – more guarded when I spoke. He was, I now realised, expert in tying his listener up in the social convention that we meet lies with polite silence. But why – what possible psychological purpose could his behaviour serve?

We wrestled with this question for the next year of his treatment. We explored the idea that his lying was a way of controlling others, or compensating for a sense of inferiority. We talked about his parents – his father was a surgeon and his mother had been a schoolteacher until her death, just before Philip's twelfth birthday.

And then, one day, Philip described a memory from

childhood which had seemed too trivial to mention until then. From the age of three, he used to share a bedroom with his twin brothers, who slept in cots nearby. He sometimes woke in the middle of the night to the sounds of people shouting as they left the pub across the road. He was often aware of a need to pee, and knew that he should get up and walk down the hall, but he would stay in bed, motionless.

'I used to wet my bed as a child,' Philip told me. He described crumpling up his damp pyjamas and pushing them deep into the covers, only to find them at bedtime under his pillow, washed and neatly folded. He never discussed it with his mother and, to the best of his knowledge, she never told anyone, including his father, about his bedwetting. 'He'd have been furious with me,' Philip said. 'I guess she thought I'd outgrow it. And I did, when she died.'

Philip could not remember being alone with his mother. For most of his childhood she had been busy taking care of the twins. He had no memory of ever talking with her on his own; one of his brothers or his father – someone – was always there. His bedwetting and her silence gradually developed into a private conversation – something only they shared. When his mother died, this conversation abruptly came to an end. And so Philip began to improvise another version of their exchange. He told lies that would make a mess and then hoped that his listener would say nothing, becoming, like his mother, a partner in a secret world.

Philip's lying was not an attack upon intimacy – though it sometimes had that effect. It was his way of keeping the closeness he had known, his way of holding on to his mother.

On not being in a couple

Michael D. telephoned me to arrange an appointment. 'I was in analysis with Dr H.,' he said.

It's the policy of my professional society that each member designates another psychoanalyst to wind up his or her practice – look after patients and carefully dispose of any confidential notes or correspondence – in the event of the analyst's sudden death. I'd agreed to look after Dr H.'s affairs, but when his death came it wasn't unexpected. He'd known he was dying of lung cancer and, in the months before he died, he wound up his practice himself. A few weeks before his death, he told me, 'My patients are settled, you shouldn't be hearing from any of them.' So when Michael D. rang me, almost two years later, I was somewhat surprised.

We agreed on a time to meet. I was just about to put down the receiver when he said, 'You don't remember me, do you?'

'I'm sorry,' I said.

'There's no reason you should remember me.' He told me that we had met before, almost twenty years ago; he was twenty-seven then. 'You didn't have a vacancy, you referred me to Dr H.'

As he spoke, I began to recall our meeting. We met for a consultation, just before his wedding day. I couldn't remember his face but I had a picture of him in jeans, T-shirt and tennis shoes, and that there was something self-conscious, boyish about him. What I did remember was the way he entered my room, holding a single sheet of lined paper. As he sat down he said, 'I've made a couple of notes.' The sheet appeared to have been folded and refolded.

From time to time, he consulted the paper, on which he'd listed questions for me – 'Should I let her keep the engagement ring?' 'Do I tell my best friends that I'm having doubts about my sexuality?' 'I have to give the guests some explanation, I don't want to lie – what do I say to people?' 'Do I have to telephone everyone myself or can Mum and Dad do it for me?'

Thinking back, I couldn't remember how I'd handled these questions. I did tell him that I thought he was very anxious, and that having those questions written out helped him to feel less confused, safer. Over the two hours we talked, he never let go of the paper.

Gradually, my experience of the paper changed. Perhaps it was the fact of him clutching it so tightly, but it felt less and less like a wall between us and more like a worn teddy bear that must be carried everywhere. At the end of the consultation, as he was putting his coat on, I heard myself ask him – like a father making sure his toddler has not left behind some beloved toy – if he'd remembered his piece of paper.

'Yes, I do remember you now,' I said. I told him I looked forward to seeing him again. We said goodbye and hung up.

After fetching Michael's assessment notes, I sat down at my desk and began to read. The pages more or less confirmed what I remembered.

Two days before coming to see me, he'd called off his wedding. Everything had happened suddenly. The previous weekend he and his fiancée, Claire, had attended a friend's wedding. Driving back to London, he became convinced that at some point, after having children, he would wake up and discover that he was gay. As Claire napped in the passenger seat, he found himself silently repeating, 'I'm not gay, I'm not gay, I'm not gay.' After a sleepless night, he told Claire he couldn't marry her, he didn't know who he was or what he wanted, maybe he was gay.

I asked him why he thought he was gay; was he having sex with a man? No, he replied. Did he fantasise about having sex with men? No, he said. Had he *ever* had sex with a man or *ever* had sexual fantasies about men? No, again. When I asked about his fiancée, he told me that he had been with Claire for three years and they'd moved in together recently. Yes, they did have sex regularly, four or five times a week. 'Do you find yourself thinking about men while you have sex with Claire?' I asked. No, he answered.

'I'm sorry,' I said. 'I don't understand. Why do you think you're gay?'

'So you don't think I'm gay?' he asked.

'I'm trying to understand why *you* think you're gay.'

'I worry that I'll discover I'm gay – after I've had children. It's a huge responsibility having children.'

'Are you worried that you may have sexual feelings towards your children?' I asked.

'No, not at all,' he replied.

From my notes it was clear we'd gone round and round like this for some time. Michael seemed to have some deep anxiety about himself, something he was convinced had to do with his sexuality, but I couldn't get a clear sense of what it was that worried him. He told me that he was a late starter, that Claire was his first and only girlfriend. At one point he told me that he found her passion embarrassing, but he couldn't explain further. And while everything Michael told me seemed to have some possible significance, I couldn't understand what he meant when he said that he was worried about his sexuality.

In my notes I recorded the thought that he seemed unable to bear the loss that marriage entails. I meant by this not only the loss of being a child, but also the loss of certain avenues that had been open to him but would now close. I was also struck by his immaturity; he was positively adolescent in his lack of empathy. He didn't seem to have much sense of the pain that he had caused his fiancée. From his description of events, it was clear she was in a state of shock.

He told me that his parents and friends all thought that Claire was a wonderful girl – intelligent and warm. He agreed. They were convinced he would lose her if he didn't propose. He found himself telling her that he wanted children and marriage, he had proposed, and they had found a home and were planning their wedding. He'd done these things because he thought this was what he should do, what he should *want* to do, but here he was, several weeks before his wedding – feeling that he couldn't go forward.

I wanted to think that it took courage to call off the wedding, but his stopping seemed almost as unthinking as his going forward. And the business about his sexuality wasn't quite right either – I suspected that it was the only excuse he believed would be accepted by those around him.

It was clear he was desperate to stop the wedding, but he couldn't say why and I couldn't figure out why. In my notes I concluded that he was breaking down into depression and needed to be helped immediately. He needed an experienced therapist who could help him get a better sense of the cause of his depression, and get a clearer picture of his underlying worries.

There was one further point in my notes, and this may have been the reason why I didn't recognise his voice on the telephone – I felt that I hadn't made good contact with him.

During a consultation, I have to gather information – the patient's life story, the history of his problem – but the most important thing is that the patient should leave our first meeting feeling heard. At the end of this meeting, he should feel that what he came to say, needed to say, has been said, listened to and thought about. In almost all consultations there is a moment when things click, when both people feel there has been an understanding. When that happens, and it can occur at almost any point in the meeting, patient and analyst have a sense that the consultation is over, the thing that was needed has been done – but that hadn't happened with Michael.

I'd had a number of thoughts and I'd put them to him, but in the end I was left feeling that nothing really seemed to make an impact. When it was time to say goodbye, I felt vaguely defeated. I comforted myself with the thought that Michael was not so interested in being heard as in getting something from me – he wanted to end his engagement and he seemed to want my permission. I felt he wanted me to say something to take back to his fiancée and parents, a sick note, excusing him from the wedding, for ever.

The only other document in the file was a photocopy of my letter, describing the consultation and referring Michael to Dr H. 'Who knows?' I had written. 'Perhaps he just needs to meet the right person.'

Sitting at my desk, closing the file, I wondered – what had become of Michael during the intervening years? Was he now married with children? And what had stopped him from marrying Claire? I returned the file to the cabinet and closed my office for the night.

A few days later, as planned, Michael arrived for his appointment. He took off his suit jacket and sat down in the chair. As he looked around the room, I caught myself looking at his left hand to see if he was wearing a wedding ring. He wasn't. 'We both have a few more white hairs,' he said to me.

We were silent for a moment. 'How can I help?' I asked.

He sat still and then said, 'One of the things that Dr H. and I figured out was that psychoanalysis can't really help me. To be honest, my analysis with Dr H. was a bit of a failure – but that failure was worth something in itself.'

I told him I wasn't sure I understood what he meant.

For a moment he seemed lost in contemplation of something visible only to him and then he said, 'Do you know the story of Kafka and Felice Bauer? For five years, Kafka was intensely involved with Bauer, sometimes sending her several letters a day. She lived in Berlin, he lived in Prague – not a great distance even then, but during the five years they were engaged, they met only ten times, often for no more than an hour or two.' If you read Kafka's letters, Michael said, it's clear that he was usually distraught – anxious about where Felice was going, who she was seeing, what she was eating or wearing. Kafka wanted instant replies to his letters, and he was furious when he didn't get them. He proposed twice and broke it off twice – the wedding never took place. Michael said that for Kafka, separation from Bauer was unbearable. 'The only thing more disturbing was her presence.

'Kafka got into that sort of relationship over and over again,' he told me. 'Nowadays, we'd say he was schizoid or suffered some mild form of Asperger's, but those words give no sense of the central thing. The person he most avoided was the person upon whom he was the most dependent – the person he most wanted.

'That's my story – with Claire, with Dr H. As time went on, the more I depended on Dr H., the more I felt I needed his help, the more I found myself skipping sessions and wanting to end the analysis altogether.'

He told me that when he started with Dr H. he was depressed – ashamed of the way he had called off the wedding, embarrassed by the things he had told people. He gave up his research fellowship in maths and got a job in banking, doing computer modelling. After about six months, he had found a new flat, and started to enjoy his job – 'I felt a bit better. Because therapy had gone so well at first, it took some time before either of us realised some obvious things: like my need to control the distance between us. Normally, people get closer and closer over time. I can't do this. My trust doesn't seem to deepen – not much anyway.'

The situation became clear following another break-up with a girlfriend. He'd been in a relationship with a woman who lived in New York. Most of the relationship was over the phone. Each weekday, when she came home from work, and just before he went to bed, Michael rang her. They saw each other once every three months. 'She thought we should see more of each other – I thought so too. Isn't that what's supposed to happen? But I just couldn't do it – we talked about my fear of intimacy, my fear of commitment, my fear of becoming a father. When she offered to move here, I freaked out – it was like it had been with Claire. I just couldn't do it, and we broke up.

'I think that Dr H. found it hard to believe that I was genuinely happier on my own – I found it hard to see at first. Like him, I believed that I had some sort of psychological block preventing me from wanting intimacy,' he said.

I asked him if he and Dr H. had come to any conclusions about why he felt this way.

'I could tell you a lot of different things, but the fact is, when I'm in a couple, I feel I'm disappearing, dying – losing my mind.'

As he spoke, I felt increasingly uncomfortable. I recognised that my inkling during our original consultation – that he wanted a sick note, excusing him from the wedding, for ever – was correct, but I had brushed it aside with my quip to Dr H., 'Perhaps he just needs to meet the right person.'

Almost as if he were reading my mind Michael said, 'A lot of people, especially psychoanalysts, assume that happiness can only be found in a couple – but not all of us are made for relationships.'

'You feel I misjudged you, got it wrong in our first consultation?' I asked.

'You were trying to figure out what went wrong between me and Claire. I came away thinking that you were perplexed, but well-meaning. Most people think I'm shy, that I'm anxious or have low self-esteem. You didn't think that, but you did think that therapy would help me get into a relationship – and that was wrong.'

He leaned forward. 'Don't feel bad, it's a mistake everyone makes and I still sometimes make about myself. But the thing is, the minute I feel I've found the right distance, the rules change, and it feels the other person is too close.

'Love can't change what's wrong with me,' Michael said, 'because love feels threatening. It's the thing that made me break down before my wedding. Being loved is the problem, because love is a demand – when you're loved, someone wants more of you.'

'This is the thing you think I didn't see – that psychoanalysts don't see.'

'Yes, but it took me a long time to see what's right for me too – who I am – and accept it.'

I heard the voices of passers-by on the pavement outside

my window. 'I'm not sure I understand what you want from me,' I said. 'How can I help?'

'I miss Dr H.,' he replied. 'I miss our conversations. He helped me to find the words to describe this – and telling it to you now makes me feel better, less lonely. I can't do intimacy, but I can feel lonely. I'd like to come and see you when I need to.'

I waited to hear if there was something more Michael wanted to say.

'Can I do that?' he asked. 'Would that be OK?'

And that is what we arranged.

A passion for ignorance

I long suspected my patient's husband was having an affair but, of course, I couldn't know for certain.

A few years after qualifying, when I was thirty-nine years old, I took on a patient I'll call Francesca L. She came to see me on the recommendation of her GP, suffering with post-partum depression. Little by little, over the course of the first year of her psychoanalysis, the depression fell away. But disagreements with her husband – probably as a result of their inability to think as a couple – caused her unhappiness and left her feeling restless.

I can only know what my patients tell me, and yet, during those first two years of Francesca's analysis, I couldn't help but think that her husband, Henry, was unfaithful. To begin with, he'd had a number of affairs during his first marriage; he'd left his wife and ten-year-old son to marry Francesca. Then there were a number of small, apparently inconsequential details that rang alarm bells with me. Every evening after work, Henry went to his health club for a swim, but on two occasions, when Francesca went to the club in the hope of finding him, he wasn't there. There were the telephone calls too – calls at odd times, urgent calls that had to be taken in another room, calls that caused Henry to drop everything and go out for two or three hours.

In one session, quite innocently, Francesca described ringing Henry's office. A colleague had answered his phone. 'He put his hand over the mouthpiece but I heard him shout: "Hey Shagger, it's for you."'

I waited and when Francesca didn't speak I asked what this meant to her.

'Nothing – I just thought it was funny. Laddish,' she said.

I was silent.

'Maybe it was even a compliment,' she said.

'Aren't you a bit curious why his colleague called him "Shagger"?' I asked.

'No, not especially. They all talk like that.'

The stories Francesca told me left me feeling anxious for her. Over time, session by session, I became increasingly frustrated with her lack of curiosity. I couldn't believe that she wouldn't want to check that Henry had used his swimming things, or search his wallet for out-of-the-ordinary receipts. She wasn't just passive; she seemed to work at keeping herself ignorant. I tried in various ways to raise this issue, but I was unsure just how far to push her.

Some nights, I found it hard to sleep. I would wake up, drink a glass of water, return to bed and lie awake, falling asleep for a few hours at dawn. I was angry because of something that had happened in my own life – and, as a result, there were times when I thought that I might be putting something of my own problems into Francesca's analysis. Just before the start of her therapy, I had gone through a difficult period with a girlfriend. There had been telephone calls – more than once I'd answered our telephone and the caller had hung up. Away for the weekend at a psychoanalytic conference in Copenhagen, I rang home late one Saturday night and my girlfriend didn't pick up. When I got home, she told me that she had felt unwell on Saturday morning, unplugged the phone and took a nap and then forgot to plug it in. 'I'm sorry,' she said, 'I only remembered on Sunday.' A month later, we broke up and I moved out – it was only when I unpacked my clothes and hung them up in the closet that I became aware of a man's shirt that did not belong to me. Lying in bed, thinking about how I'd been deceived, I could not sleep.

A few weeks after our exchange about the nickname 'Shagger', Francesca heard her mobile phone ping – a text message. She picked it up off the kitchen table and read: xxx. It wasn't at all like Henry to text a kiss, let alone three. Then she realised that it wasn't her telephone – she and Henry had identical phones – it was his. Who, she asked him, was sending him a kiss? He told her that it was probably a mistake or one of the guys at the office mucking about – he didn't recognise the number.

'Did you look at his other text messages? Or his call log?' I asked her.

'No, I thought I did what you wanted me to do – I asked him what it was all about and he explained it,' she said. 'I thought you'd be pleased with me.'

My heart sank. It was increasingly clear that Francesca felt compelled to tell me stories that would lead me to believe that Henry was unfaithful. But when I tried to discuss the possibility that he might be having an affair, she would abruptly become obtuse. None of this made any sense, and yet Francesca was so comfortable with this inconsistency that I thought it must make some deeper sense to her – but what?

For some months, we returned to this problem. Of course, I considered the possibility that my over-identification with Francesca caused me to misread her situation, see my betrayal in her marriage – but this didn't make sense. She wasn't inventing Henry's actions. Was I supposed to have her worries, so that she didn't? Perhaps she was trying to hook me into thinking about her as a victim, a waif – but for what possible reason? We looked at her relationship with her parents, which had always been something of a mystery to me. They seemed formal and distant. Preoccupied with his small picture-framing business, her father worked long hours. I noticed too that even though they lived nearby,

Francesca's mother hardly ever visited. She took little interest in her granddaughter, Lottie.

So when Francesca's mother asked her to lunch on her own, she suspected her mother had something important to tell her – money worries, cancer? Instead, her mother told her that for more than thirty years, Francesca's father and his business partner, June, had been having an affair. Francesca's parents were trying to work it out. Her father was selling his share in the business; they were also cutting June and her husband out of their personal lives. But her mother was still uncertain about what she really wanted to do.

I asked Francesca how her mother discovered the affair.

'She didn't,' Francesca said. 'June's husband told her. He'd known for years. He said something to my mum assuming that she did too.'

Francesca was not at all surprised by her mother's news. She recalled a number of moments when she saw her father and June behaving in a way that suggested they were lovers. She told me that one day after school, when she was fifteen or sixteen, on impulse, she went by the shop. Looking through the window before entering, she saw the two of them in the empty display area, bent over a table, their heads almost touching, looking at a picture. She watched as her father put his arm around June's waist. A moment later, her father looked up, his eye caught Francesca's – he blanched and abruptly stepped back. Recovering, he bounded towards the front door, and with a sweep of his arm and a too-loud voice he invited her in.

When I heard about her father's affair I thought it could help to explain Francesca's blindness towards Henry's behaviour – that, for some yet unknown reason, she had married a version of her father; she'd taken up her mother's role. A few days later, after another one of Francesca's descriptions of Henry's manoeuvrings – he'd been out most of the night 'with a client' – I pointed out to her just how similar her marriage was to her parents'. 'Henry seems to have found a wife who – like your mum – closes her eyes to any evidence of infidelity.'

'But I'm nothing like her,' Francesca replied. 'I did tell my mum – I told her about the time I saw them in the shop. Plenty of times I asked her, didn't it worry her that Daddy and June were constantly together? And she always said, "No, they're just business partners." I knew there was something going on but nothing I said could convince her.'

It seemed to me that Francesca wasn't simply reprising her mother's role as the betrayed wife – she was also putting me in the very same position she'd been in as a child. Was she, unconsciously, involuntarily, communicating to me the frustration and isolation she'd once felt?

Francesca told me, 'At some level, my mum must've known but she couldn't let herself know. Her whole world would have fallen apart. She'd have lost her family, her home. She would have had a breakdown if she wasn't in denial.' All the same, her mother's solution had consequences.

Francesca's mother had accepted her husband's version of events over her daughter's. In not responding to what Francesca was trying to tell her, she'd created an impossible distance between the two of them.

At the beginning of Francesca's third year of psycho-analysis, Henry's job sent him to Paris for the year. He had arranged to take the Eurostar early Monday morning, stay in the company flat during the week, and return to London on Friday evening. But since moving, Henry had stayed in Paris on a number of weekends – he'd missed Lottie's birthday in January, Valentine's weekend in February. In March, they decided that Francesca and Lottie would spend Easter with him in the Paris flat.

In our first session after the Easter break, Francesca told me about the visit.

'Friday evening, we got to Gare du Nord. Henry was there waiting for us. We took a taxi back to his flat in the Marais and all ate dinner together, and that felt good – being a family again. We put Lottie to bed and then went into the kitchen to tidy up and have a glass of wine.

'I opened the dishwasher and immediately knew some-thing wasn't right, but for a second I didn't know what it was.

'Then the hushed phone calls, the nickname "Shagger", missing Lottie's birthday – all of it made sense. It was like those spy games. There's always a point when you've decoded enough letters in the message – you haven't worked out every one – but suddenly the whole message is absolutely clear. It was like that. I didn't need any more information. In the dishwasher were two coffee cups, two small breakfast plates, two butter knives, two glasses, and two teaspoons, all where they should be – not just thrown in like Henry always does. It was as if she'd left me a note.

'I said to him, "Who loaded the dishwasher?—Tell me, who loaded the dishwasher?"'

On intimacy

When Joshua B. rang, less than a year after his psychoanalysis had ended, I felt uneasy. 'Do you have any time this week?' he asked.

He came by a few hours later. 'New curtains,' he said, looking around the room. Then he sat down. 'I'm a dick, a complete dick,' he told me. 'I'm in a terrible situation, and I don't know how to get myself out.'

'What's happened?' I asked.

'Oh, don't worry – everything's fine with Emma and the baby. They're OK.' He sipped water from a bottle he'd brought with him. 'But I've been seeing this girl.' He looked at me, trying to gauge my response. 'Are you surprised?'

'Why don't you tell me about it?'

Joshua had been seeing a girl named Alison, a twenty-two-year-old escort he'd found over the Internet. For the last few months, he'd seen her several times a week; he phoned or texted her daily. He was trying to help her change her life. He'd bought her a laptop, and taken her clothes-shopping before a recent job interview.

'Last week I tried to end it with her. Our deal was I'd help her, but only if she stopped working. Then I found out she hadn't stopped. So I broke it off. But she called me the next day and told me that she missed me and she needed to see me. I caved. I'm not an idiot – I know that I'll lose everything if I don't stop. But I can't.'

As he spoke, I considered his timing. He and his wife, Emma, had just had a baby boy. Had Joshua turned to a prostitute because he needed to separate love and sex? Was he trying to protect Emma from desires that he thought were dirty or wrong? I started to explain these thoughts to Joshua, but he cut me off. 'No, Emma and I still have sex. I've never had sex with Alison.'

'Wait,' I said, 'I don't understand.'

'The first time I met Alison I went for sex. I paid her and then she told me that she'd double-booked – did I mind waiting round the corner at the cafe for an hour? I waited, thinking she'd never turn up, but she did.' He told me that they talked for a long time, that she was great, remarkable really. She had offered to give him back his money but he told her to keep it. They met again the next day, and continued talking.

'There's no sex at all?' I asked.

'She kisses me when I turn up and when I leave. She's very

physical – touching me when she talks, sometimes we hold hands – but we haven't had sex.'

'But you pay her when you see her?'

'I give her money, but I don't *pay* her. I buy her things she needs, give her money for her mother, who's ill – I'm trying to help her. For a while I thought I'd have sex with her if I didn't have to pay for it, but now I feel that would be wrong too. My hope is she'll leave prostitution, and I'll have launched her into the world, and that she'll love me for what I've done for her.'

Over the years, I've seen several male patients become obsessed with prostitutes. The pick-up, put-down nature of the experience – the avoidance of dependence and emotional intimacy – makes the sex feel safer. And of course prostitution is a monetary transaction, and this inspires fantasy. But for Joshua, Alison meant something else.

'Listen to the words you're using,' I told him. '"Launch her into the world", "love you for what you've done for her." You sound a little like a mother talking about a baby.'

Joshua took another sip of water. 'So I'm doing all of this because I wish I was a mother too? I envy my wife?'

I didn't answer. It might be true that he envied his wife her relationship to their son; this would explain something of the nature of his relationship to Alison, particularly Joshua's mothering and the absence of sex. And yet it also seemed possible that he was acting out of envy for his son. In trying to seduce Alison from prostitution he might be endeavouring to steal a woman away from men – as he felt his son had stolen his wife from him. 'Have you gone to prostitutes before?' I asked.

'No, never,' he said. He told me that he and Emma had been together for eight years and he'd never been unfaithful to her, until this. 'Did I tell you she calls the baby by the nickname she used to call me?'

'You're telling me that you've always been faithful to Emma, but something's changed. I think you're betraying your wife because you feel betrayed.'

Joshua leaned forward. 'Do you remember the holiday Emma and I took two years ago, during the summer break? We rented that great cottage by the sea for almost a whole month. No Internet or television. A guy in a van turned up twice a week with fresh fish. I cooked for us every night. Emma fell in love with the kids next door, and that was sort of it. She wanted kids, then we wanted kids – isn't that what we're all supposed to want?'

'But perhaps when you agreed to having a baby, you didn't know how it would make you feel.'

'I didn't know it would make me feel so lonely.'

Joshua *was* lonely. Perhaps more than that, he was jealous of the closeness his wife and son shared. Unable to imagine a way in, Joshua could not find his place as a father. He experienced this incapacity as his wife abandoning him. What he claimed brightly as an act of folly was really an act of revenge.

The bigger the front

Boarding a flight from New York to San Francisco, settling into my seat, I find I'm sharing the row with an attractive, well-dressed woman. She has the window, I have the aisle. The seat between us is empty. I volunteer to move so her two boys, who're in the next row over, can join her. She laughs, and tells me that I clearly don't have teenage kids – 'They'd prefer to be sitting even further away.'

She asks about me. I ask about her. I ask if she's going on vacation. No, she tells me, she's on her way to visit her mom. She adjusts her necklace. 'It'll be the first time I've seen her in sixteen years – since my parents cut me out of their lives.'

Her comment has the effect I think she wants it to have – I want to know what happened.

Abby tells me that eighteen years earlier she met a guy named Patrick. They were medical students together. Although she was Jewish and he was Catholic, she believed that her parents would eventually come to accept him. 'My family was never particularly observant, and Patrick is really someone special.'

Abby's dad, who is also a doctor, was extremely upset by the idea of her blond boyfriend – he made terrible racist comments about Patrick. When Abby and Patrick became engaged, he told her that if she actually went ahead and married him, he'd have nothing more to do with her. He told her he'd sit shiva – go into mourning.

'I don't know if he actually sat shiva, but on the day I married Patrick he stopped speaking to me.' As usual, her mother followed her father's lead. For several years, Abby sent birthday cards and Chanukkah presents to her parents, but, after the birth of her first child, when they didn't respond to the birth announcement, she just gave up.

There were times, especially during the first few years of her marriage, when she thought she was going crazy. Whenever she and Patrick had an argument, she found herself thinking that she should've married someone more like her, someone Jewish – maybe her dad was right. She talked to a psychotherapist about all this, but that didn't really help. 'We couldn't make sense of what had happened – was my dad jealous of Patrick? Jealous of me? His behaviour made no sense at all.

'Then, out of the blue, a couple of months ago, I get a call from my mom telling me that she and my dad are getting a divorce. My mom's discovered that he's been having an affair with Kathy, his receptionist. She's worked for my dad for twenty-five years. Apparently, they've been having an affair since I graduated from high school. Surprise, surprise – Kathy is Catholic, and blonde.

'And then I got it,' Abby says, *'the bigger the front, the bigger the back.'*

Psychoanalysts call this 'splitting'– an unconscious strategy that aims to keep us ignorant of feelings in ourselves that we're unable to tolerate. Typically, we want to see ourselves as good, and put those aspects of ourselves that we find shameful into another person or group.

Splitting is one way we have of getting rid of self-knowledge. When Abby's father cut her off, he was trying to cut himself off from those hateful aspects of himself that he could not bear. In the short term, this gives us some relief – 'I'm not bad, you are.' But in denying and projecting a part of ourselves into another, we come to regard these negative aspects as outside of our control. At its extreme, splitting renders the world an unsettling, even dangerous place – rather than recognise his devils as his own, Abby's father meets them, as if for the first time, in his daughter.

Imagine his predicament – it was unbearable for him to think that he'd fallen in love with someone outside of his religion. Able to locate the problem in Abby, he lost awareness of it in himself. He continues his affair with Kathy but because he lacks an internal experience of his own feelings and actions, he's lost the best means he has of making sense of himself or his daughter.

I like Abby's phrase *the bigger the front, the bigger the back* – it's more telling than the psychoanalytic term. Splitting is thinner, less dynamic; it suggests two separate, disjointed things. Abby's saying captures the fact that front and back are a part of each other.

Ever since hearing Abby's story, whenever I hear about a family-values politician who's caught with his pants down, or some homosexuality-is-a-sin evangelist found in bed with a male prostitute, I think – *the bigger the front, the bigger the back.*

Loving

At home

The first time I saw Professor James R. was on the morning of Halloween. My children were still in their pyjamas, and they told me that while I was downstairs at work they were going to make a chocolate cake with Mummy, and decorate it with icing-sugar ghosts.

The sounds of my wife clearing away the last of the breakfast things and the first notes of my daughter's piano practice faded away as I walked downstairs to my consulting room, and closed the door behind me. I turned on the lights, adjusted the thermostat and put the newspaper in the waiting room. It was ten to nine.

When he'd rung to arrange an assessment, Professor R. hadn't sounded particularly anxious – my intuition was that he wouldn't be early, probably right on time. I sat in my chair, looked again at his name and address in my diary, and closed my eyes. It's difficult to describe my feelings in the moments just before a consultation – the mixture of anticipation, curiosity and vague unease.

At two or three minutes past nine, the doorbell rang. The man standing on my doorstep was taller, more solid, than his voice had led me to expect. 'Mr Grosz?'

After he settled himself in the chair opposite me, I asked him, 'How can I help?'

He told me that he wasn't sure I could; he wasn't sure anyone could. He started to tell me about himself. He was seventy-one years old; until his retirement he'd been professor at a large London teaching hospital. He'd done well professionally, but he didn't understand why. He told me that because he spoke slowly, people often thought he was intelligent. 'I'm not particularly intelligent.'

He described his forty-four-year marriage to Isabel, a family doctor. He told me about their children – two girls then two boys. The girls were married with children of their own; the boys weren't married but were well settled in their careers. 'It's been a long haul, hard at times, but I've no real worries about any of them.'

He paused. 'Isabel and I have only seen the marital therapist once, and she thought it would be a good idea for me to come and see you. She said that you'd be able to help me find a therapist. But I don't know what she's told you about me.'

I told him what the marital therapist had said – that she'd thought it best to let him tell me about himself.

Before I could say more, he added, 'Did she tell you that I'm gay?'

The simple story, he said, was this: when he married Isabel, he put his sexuality in a box. Then, two years ago, just after his father died, 'I took it out again.' He'd been on a visit to New York, to see his daughter and her family, and found himself in a midtown Manhattan sauna. 'For the first time in my life, I felt myself.'

His relationship with the man he'd met in the sauna was short-lived, but he'd had two other boyfriends since then. 'I'm obviously not young, so I've had to learn about Viagra. But this isn't just about sex – I know this is important to me.'

I asked him if he was telling me that he'd never had sex with a man before then.

'That's right,' he said. He'd been sexually attracted to men all his life. He'd always known he was gay and assumed when he went to university that he would meet a man and that would be that, but it never happened. 'There were some brave people who were openly gay, but I wasn't one of them.'

He leaned forward in his chair. He told me that he and his wife were in medical school together – 'she was then, is now, my best friend' – and after graduation they got married. Yes, he'd tried to raise the subject with Isabel on several occasions over the years but these attempts didn't go anywhere.

A couple of months ago, he'd told her about the man he was seeing. She was, of course, upset, but understanding. There were several dreadful weeks before they agreed to see a marital therapist. He didn't know what to do – he wanted to stay in the life he'd built with Isabel, but he didn't know how. 'That's why I'm here.'

On some days he was convinced they should sell their large home and buy two small houses, one for him and one for Isabel, so that they could each lead their own lives. But on other days he thought the problem was something more fundamental, one of intimacy. 'I have the dreadful feeling that I could choose to be with a man and soon discover that I couldn't be close to him either.'

I asked him what he meant.

He told me that Isabel was good with people, he wasn't. He didn't really know how she had put up with him all these years – it was a family joke that he was at his best with the anaesthetised. 'I'm awkward. Some people like that, some don't. I always seem to say the unsaid thing, the thing everyone's thinking but no one wants to say.'

I tried not to show it, but I think he sensed how I heard this – that he could say the unsaid thing about others, but not himself. Did he make it awkward for others so that he didn't feel awkward? As I was thinking about this he asked, 'How's psychotherapy going to help me resolve this?'

I told him that I wasn't yet sure in what way psychotherapy might help him.

He told me that he liked to reach a decision and then

act – and now, he couldn't decide what to do. Nobody had ever thought of him as confused, yet that's how he was now. Both staying and leaving could, at different times, feel the right thing to do. His children didn't know he was gay, and he didn't want them to know. He didn't want them to hate him, to think the worst of him.

I told him that I understood him to be saying that he didn't want to do anything he'd later regret.

He agreed. 'Sometimes it feels right that I leave. I've never felt completely myself with Isabel.' He described a Sunday afternoon he'd spent lying in his boyfriend's arms. 'We were in the bedroom listening to a CD. When it finished, I didn't let go and he just continued to hold me. We lay there for most of the afternoon, until I wanted to get up. I'd never known anything like that before.'

'And you don't want to give that up.'

'Exactly – I don't think I can give it up.'

'Why now?' I asked.

He told me he wasn't sure. Perhaps it had something to do with where he and Isabel were in their lives. Since medical school he'd spent most of his life caring for others. One after another Isabel's parents, then his parents became ill, required their help, then died: breast cancer, colon cancer, heart disease, pancreatic cancer. His oldest daughter had had a difficult childhood – she was dyslexic, never got on with her teachers, and had been caught shoplifting. But all this was in the past – his parents were gone and his children were now fine. 'It may sound selfish, but now I want to feel someone loves me, not that they're just dutifully caring for me.'

We were silent for a few minutes.

'It's terrible, but I felt relieved when my father died. He was awful.' While his father was well respected in the community, a GP and local councillor, he was impossible to live with. He was a professional do-gooder, and everyone thought he was wonderful. But he was prone to sudden rages. 'He'd quickly recover but I'd go on shaking inside for the longest time. We could see him building up to one of his explosions, but there was no way of calming him.'

What was worse was something else – how to describe it? – his father's lack of interest in him. 'I mostly remember him not being there – I remember him going to his practice before I left for school. It was clear I was, in some way, just too much for him. It felt like he couldn't wait to get away from me.'

As he spoke, I saw again his memory, his pleasure in holding a man – his boyfriend stilled, calm in his arms – and also being held for as long as he wanted. And I asked him if he thought part of the power of being held by a man was that it undid the rejection, the pain he'd suffered from his father.

'I feel my father looked into me and he didn't like what he saw. That afternoon I felt the opposite of that – I felt at home.'

We were both silent for a moment then he said, 'I imagine

my story isn't very typical – there can't be many men who come to you, who change direction like this, now, at my age. But there it is.' He made a small gesture, turning his palms upwards. 'There it is.'

For a long time we sat together, neither of us speaking, and I thought about the journey of his marriage – I imagined, almost like a series of photographs, him and his wife at medical school, their wedding, the births of their children and deaths of their parents, their years together. I saw the annual cycle of birthday parties and holidays. I thought of Professor R. and his wife as students – so much they couldn't know then, so much they couldn't foresee.

Then, perhaps it was some remote noise from upstairs, maybe it was the piano or the sound of voices, that made me think of my own wife and children, and I imagined a similar series of photographs from our life – our births, our deaths. What lay ahead for us?

Professor R. sighed, and I asked him what he'd been thinking about in the silence.

'I was thinking that if my wife can live with me as I am, I want to stay with her and continue to see my boyfriend. If she can do that, that's what I want.'

We stopped shortly after that, and, as we'd agreed, I referred Professor R. to a psychotherapist whose work I admired and whose consulting room was near Professor R.'s home. I did not see him again but I found myself thinking about this consultation from time to time – I wasn't sure why.

Two years later, I was sitting in a local cafe waiting for my wife. Glancing through a copy of *The Times* that had been left on the table, my eye was caught by the sight of Professor R.'s name and photograph among the obituaries. There was an account of a distinguished career, as well as tributes from friends and from colleagues. The obituary concluded by saying that his wife was with him when he died, peacefully, at home.

How paranoia can relieve suffering and prevent a catastrophe

Amanda P., a twenty-eight-year-old single woman, returns home to London after a work trip to America. She has been in New York for ten days. She lives alone. She sets her briefcase down on her doorstep, and, as she turns her key in the lock, an idea takes hold. 'I had this fantasy – I saw it like a film: turning the key triggers some sort of detonator and the whole flat blows up, the door exploding off its hinges towards me, killing me instantly. I was imagining that terrorists had been in my flat and had carefully primed a bomb to kill me. Why would I have such a crazy fantasy?'

Or take, for example, these fleeting paranoid fantasies: a woman is walking down the street, smiling to herself; Simon A. – an attractive and well-dressed architect – becomes convinced that she is laughing at his clothes. Or there is Lara G. – her boss has asked her to come to his office at the end of the work day. As they have not spoken for several weeks,

Lara is certain that she is going to be fired. Instead, she is dumbfounded when she's offered a promotion and a pay increase. Then there is George N. who, while he is showering, occasionally fears that the shower curtain will be pulled back and he will be murdered, 'à la Hitchcock's *Psycho*. My heart pounds,' George told me. 'For an instant I have this terrible panic that I am not alone in my flat – that someone has come to murder me.'

Most, if not all, of us have had irrational fantasies at one time or another. And yet we rarely acknowledge them – even to spouses or close friends. We find them difficult, even impossible, to talk about. We don't know what they signify or say about us. Are they a sign that we're breaking down? Momentarily mad? There are various psychological theories about why paranoid fantasies are a part of normal mental life. One theory is that paranoia allows us to rid ourselves of certain aggressive feelings. Anger is unconsciously projected: 'I don't want to hurt him, he wants to hurt me.' Another theory holds that paranoia allows us to deny our own unwanted sexual feelings: 'I don't love him, I hate him and he hates me.' Both of these descriptions may well apply, but neither seems quite sufficient.

Anyone can become paranoid – that is, develop an irrational fantasy of being betrayed, mocked, exploited or harmed – but we are more likely to become paranoid if we are insecure, disconnected, alone. Above all, paranoid fantasies are a response to the feeling that we are being treated with indifference.

In other words, paranoid fantasies are disturbing, but they are a defence. They protect us from a more disastrous emotional state – namely, the feeling that no one is concerned about us, that no one cares. The thought 'so-and-so has betrayed me' protects us from the more painful thought 'no one thinks about me'. And this is one reason why soldiers commonly suffer paranoia.

During the First World War, British soldiers in the trenches became convinced that the French farmers who continued to plough their fields behind British lines were secretly signalling the German artillery. In *The Great War and Modern Memory*, Paul Fussell documents soldiers' widespread conviction that the farmers were directing the German guns to British emplacements. Fussell writes, 'In both wars it was widely believed but never, so far as I know, proved that French, Belgians or Alsatians living just behind the line signaled the distant German artillery by fantastically elaborate, shrewd, and accurate means.' The troops saw terrifying codes in the random movements of a windmill, or in the sight of a man walking two cows into a field, or of a laundress hanging linen on a line. It is less painful, it turns out, to feel betrayed than to feel forgotten.

With old age, the likelihood of developing a serious psychological disorder decreases, and yet the chance of developing paranoia increases. In hospital, I have heard elderly men and women complain: 'The nurses here are trying to poison me.' 'I didn't misplace my glasses, my daughter has obviously stolen them.' 'You don't believe me but I can assure you: my room is bugged, they are reading my post.' 'Please take me home, I'm not safe here.' To be sure, the old are sometimes abused, tricked by family members and mistreated by caregivers, so it is important to listen carefully to their fears. But all too frequently – like the soldiers in the trenches – the elderly face death feeling forgotten. Women and men who were once attractive and important find themselves increasingly overlooked. My experience is that paranoid fantasies are often a response to the world's disregard. The paranoid knows that someone is thinking about him.

I asked Amanda P. to tell me more about arriving home from New York. 'I love my flat,' she said. 'But coming home after a trip is one of those moments when I really hate being single. I open the door and there is ten days' post on the mat, the fridge is empty, the house is cold. No one has been cooking so the place smells abandoned – it's depressing.' She paused. 'It's the exact opposite of what it was like to come home from school as a child. My mum or nan – or both – were there, making my tea. Someone was always waiting for me.'

As she spoke it became clear that Amanda P.'s momentary paranoid fantasy – of turning her key and being blown up by terrorists – was, to answer her question, not crazy at all. For a minute the fantasy frightened her, but ultimately this fear saved her from feeling alone. The thought 'someone wants to kill me' gave her an experience of being hated – but not forgotten. She existed in the mind of the terrorist. Her paranoia shielded her from the catastrophe of indifference.

On the recovery of lost feelings

When she was six years old, Emma F. fell in love with her Year 2 teacher, Miss King. Miss King wore shiny hoop earrings and bright red nail polish. She and Emma shared a fascination with fossils. Once, Emma told Miss King that she was reading *Charlotte's Web* all over again, and Miss King squeezed Emma's hand – it was one of her favourite books too.

Before breakfast, on the last Saturday of the school year, Emma sat down at the kitchen table to make a thank-you card for Miss King. She drew a picture of an ammonite on the front, then opened the card and wrote: 'Dear Miss King, you are the best teacher ever. Thank you for being my teacher. I will miss you next year. I love you more than anyone even Mummy. Love, Emma xxxxx'

When her father sat down, Emma showed him the card. 'You can't say that you love Miss King more than you love Mummy,' he told her. 'It's not true.' Emma took a pink rubber from her pencil case and began to erase the last sentence of her note. Her father stopped her. 'I can still read what you wrote,' he said. 'You need to make a new card.' And it was because of this – because he didn't want any trace of her words to remain – that Emma knew she'd done something truly wrong.

Emma soon forgot about her card and the exchange with her father. But twenty-three years later, she remembered it, during a psychoanalytic session.

That morning, Emma had been late to meet her boyfriend, Mark, for coffee. Soon after she arrived, they got into an argument about Emma's relationship with her friend Phoebe. Mark insisted it made no sense for Emma to keep seeing her friend; Phoebe always made her feel bad about herself.

'He doesn't understand why I like her,' she told me later. 'He says I'm always down after I see her.'

'Are you?' I asked.

'Mark says I am.'

'I'm not asking what Mark thinks you feel. I'm trying to figure out with you what you feel.'

'He must be right – why would he lie?'

And it was then, when I didn't immediately answer, that she remembered Miss King.

I'd been treating Emma for almost a year. She'd first come to see me because she'd become acutely depressed after beginning a PhD. She'd been prescribed antidepressants. Her psychiatrist asked me to see her after she told him that she was longing to talk to someone – 'to break through the wall that keeps me from living'.

In our first sessions, Emma described her childhood as normal, happy. But slowly, over the following months, another story surfaced. Emma's father was frequently away for work; her mother was insecure, unsure of herself. They quarrelled frequently. Just before Emma's sister was born, Emma was sent to Scotland, to her grandmother's, where she stayed for six or seven months. Without emotion Emma described returning to her parents and new baby sister, and how she missed her grandmother and cried for her at night, 'My parents have this funny story about how, when I came home, I insisted on calling my mum "lady" – I wouldn't call her "Mummy".'

As best I could tell, Emma's parents' self-esteem, their emotional equilibrium, seemed dependent on Emma behaving, achieving.

Events in Emma's early life that would ordinarily have caused a child anxiety – the first day of nursery, being forgotten outside school at pick-up time, getting lost in a department store – seemed not to have bothered her at all. My suspicion was that Emma feared being sent away again if she allowed herself to feel her own feelings. And while Emma's skill in fitting in with her parents' wishes did not prevent the development of her substantial intellectual abilities, it did stop her emotional development.

When Emma's PhD supervisor asked her to choose between two different areas of research, to tell him which area she wished to pursue and why – Emma broke down. Having to choose a direction, she had no compass, she was lost.

In the quiet of the consulting room, Emma asked, 'Why do you think I'm remembering Miss King's card now?'

'Why do you think?'

'I don't know. The conversation with my dad was like the conversation with Mark – both were telling me what I really feel, or should feel.'

Emma said that she didn't understand how people knew what they really felt. 'Most of the time, I don't know what I feel. I figure out what I *should* feel and then just act that way.'

I started to point out to Emma that she *did* know where to look: her own memories, dreams, actions. Her memory of her father came to mind as we were talking about her argu-ment with Mark – the two events felt similar to her. And in telling me that she was late again to meet Mark, she was signalling to us both her lack of enthusiasm for seeing him. But as I tried to explain my thoughts, Emma began to cry.

'Miss King,' she said, sobbing. 'Miss King.'

Later Emma would tell me that she didn't know why remembering that morning in the kitchen had made her so upset, so overemotional. 'Mum hates self-pity,' she said. I told her that I didn't think it was self-pity; it was sadness. She seemed to be crying for the self she'd lost, grieving for the little girl who wasn't allowed to have her feelings.

Why parents envy their children

Some years ago, I had a patient I'll call Amira. When she was twenty-seven years old, Amira was in a serious car accident – the car she was driving skidded into the central reservation on the M1 motorway. The accident left her physically uninjured but emotionally wrecked.

Two years after the accident, Amira was beginning to put her life back together, but finding it more and more difficult to tell her mother about her improving situation. 'I can't stand her "*Masha'Allahs*", Amira told me. '*Masha'Allah* means "God has willed it". My mother says it whenever anything good happens to me. She says it's to ward off the "evil eye" – to protect me from people's envy – and it's driving me crazy.'

Amira described a conversation with her mother about the arrangements that she and her fiancé were making for their honeymoon. 'I told her we had decided to go to Paris: "*Masha'Allah*." I started to tell her about the hotel we'd chosen:

"*Masha'Allah.*" I tried to tell her about our suite and our plans: "*Masha'Allah, masha'Allah, masha'Allah.*" I felt like throwing my mobile out the window,' Amira said. 'My happiness isn't only God's will – it's partly my accomplishment.'

It seemed to me that Amira's mother's desire to protect her daughter from other people's envy was rooted in her own feelings of envy. Amira was at first surprised by this idea. But as she thought about it, it became clear that her mother was probably missing an earlier time. Amira's mother had once told her that one of the happiest times in her life was during her first year of marriage, when she and Amira's father had lived in France. 'It can't be easy for her,' Amira admitted. 'I'm looking forward to a marriage and children, and she's a widow, looking back.' Later, Amira wondered if she had been insensitive, or had perhaps unwittingly tried to make her mother jealous.

We often envy our children their treasures – growing physical and mental strength, liveliness, joy, material comforts. But above all else, we envy our children their potential. Robert B., a fifty-five-year-old civil servant, once described to me a dream he'd had: 'I'm on a mountain. My dead grandparents are at the very top, above the clouds. They're resting in a small wooden hut, waiting for my parents who are just below the summit. I'm further down the mountain from my parents. My children are at the foot of the mountain and have just left our base camp. I hide behind a rock and my children pass me.

When I step back on to the path and see them high above me, I feel euphoric.'

Among other things, Robert's dream depicts his view of life's expedition from birth to death, from cradle (base camp) to grave (a small wooden hut). It also represents his unconscious wish to step out of time, to reverse places with his children, so that he might have an even longer future stretching out before him than they do.

For the most part, the envy I'm describing is unconscious: furtive, resistant to investigation or corroboration. We glimpse it in our dreams, but also in our slips and blunders. A mother I know, raised in poverty, was thrilled to buy her daughter a wool suit at Prada but, within hours, had accidentally put the skirt in the washing machine, ruining it. Envy often comes disguised in a correction – a father deflates his enthusiastic child with words like 'cheeky' or 'precocious'; a mother complains that her child is ungrateful: 'You don't know how lucky you are,' 'I never had a such-and-such like this.' When we envy our children we deceive ourselves – we think too little of them and too well of ourselves.

You don't have to be a parent to feel this particular envy. A sports coach can envy his athlete, a teacher can envy his student, and – it would be unfair not to include this – a psychoanalyst can envy his patient. Sometimes our patients are younger, brighter and financially more successful than we are. And it is not all that unusual that a psychoanalyst can help a patient solve a problem that the psychoanalyst himself has been struggling with unsuccessfully in his own life. Any 'parent' can get snagged by this particular form of envy.

The question is this: can we unhook ourselves by reaching an acceptance of ourselves and our place in time, so that we can enjoy our child's pleasures and successes? For at its furthest extreme, envying one's child is a great psychological misfortune, and we stand to lose both our mental equilibrium and our child.

Ten years ago, Stanley P., a seventy-seven-year-old widower and father of four, was referred to me by his family doctor. His activities were increasingly restricted – in this way, I soon saw, he avoided feeling envious of others. He did not travel and would socialise only with those for whom he felt contempt – the people he hired to do odd jobs, for example. He was uncomfortable with his children. He complained to each child about the others – about their husbands and wives, the birthday gifts they had given him, or the frequency of their telephone calls. Stanley's behaviour had caused his children gradually to withdraw from his life – and this only confirmed his sense of their selfishness.

One day Stanley described a visit from his daughter, who used to bring her husband and children to see him several times a year, but now came on her own, at most once a year. As he told me about saying goodbye to her, holding her hand in an airport cafe, Stanley became tearful. He recalled a time when she was small, and he'd stood just outside her bedroom door as she tried to read *The Tale of Mrs Tiggy-Winkle* to her teddy bear. But this memory, and his feelings of tender sadness, soon gave way to a list of grievances – about the brevity of her visit, the cheapness of her parting gift. And she was lost to him again. What remained of his feelings of love for his child stood little chance against the grand narrative that his envy had written.

On wanting the impossible

My patient, a professional middle-aged woman named Rebecca, folded her coat over the back of a chair and arranged herself on the couch. For five minutes, she was silent. Then she said, 'I'm going to have to talk about sex today.'

This was on a Monday. Rebecca had started coming to see me the year before, shortly after the death of her older sister. She was surprised by the intensity of her feelings of loss and anxiety. These feelings had lessened, but she was now more aware of her own mortality – 'I'm not living my life as fully as possible,' she told me, 'but I'm not sure what I'd like my life to be.' Her relationship with her husband seemed better but sometimes she worried she'd made the wrong choice.

Rebecca and her husband Tom had spent the previous night in – sushi, some leftover champagne, and a DVD. They took a bath together and spent a long time making love. 'I had a great orgasm,' she told me. Ordinarily, this would have guaranteed her a solid night's sleep. Instead she woke at 4.30 a.m., and, unable to get back to sleep, decided to masturbate. Soon after, she fell asleep and had what she called 'a sex dream'.

During our session, she tried to reconstruct the dream. 'It was about a man, maybe an old boyfriend from university, he was pressing against me,' she said. 'He held – no, he patted my waist. I don't remember much, just that he wanted me.' She woke up feeling bereft.

'You'd have thought the sex or the masturbation would have been enough – what's going on with me?'

We talked about the days leading up to her dream. On Saturday night, she'd had a party at a restaurant to celebrate her fiftieth birthday. Her parents had come down from Scotland. Georgia and Anne, her daughters, had helped to arrange the dinner, and had chosen the menu. Her youngest, Oliver, was to make his way to the party from his university in Sussex, but he didn't show up. Rebecca's husband had spent a good part of the evening outside the restaurant trying to reach Oliver on his mobile. 'We left his place at the table all evening,' she said. 'I didn't know whether to be worried or furious.'

Rebecca had finally reached Oliver the following afternoon. He'd told her that something important had come up at the last minute, and that the battery in his phone had been dead, so he hadn't called. Rebecca assumed that he'd simply decided to spend Saturday night with his friends. 'To be honest, I think he just couldn't be bothered,' she told me.

For Rebecca's husband, the night at the restaurant seemed to confirm his feelings of estrangement from his son. 'Tom says he's just waiting for some disaster – for the police to show up at our door,' she said. Rebecca remembered Oliver's daring, his wilfulness as a child. Once, she told me, when he was very small, he slipped out of the house while she was running his bath. She hadn't given him an ice cream after his tea and so he'd crossed a busy road to the newsagent's to get one for himself.

Listening to my patient, I began to think that her sexual behaviour was a defence, a reaction to the sadness, anger and anxiety that her son had provoked. I suspected, and she did too, that she was using sex as an antidepressant – a means of momentarily replacing emptiness and fear with the excitement of being desired. She pointed out that sex also helped to blot out disturbing thoughts – like the idea Tom had planted in her head about Oliver's recklessness one day leading the police to their door.

But this wasn't quite right – for while her sexual behaviour now looked to both of us like a way of defending herself against certain feelings, it hadn't felt like that to her at the time. Rather, she had felt the whole night that she was searching for something. Masturbation followed sex, and the dream followed the masturbation, because there was something that she wanted, not something that she wanted to get away from. She'd got out of bed feeling bereft, not depressed. But why?

What did she want?

Suddenly, jostled by a memory, she shifted on the couch.

She began to tell me about a sunny day she'd once spent in the park with Oliver and her mother. Oliver was three at the time. They were all sharing a blanket, watching the older children and their parents fly kites. Rebecca was showing her mother the Mother's Day card Ollie had made for her at nursery school. On the front of the card Oliver had carefully coloured in a steam train. On the inside of the card, where he'd clearly laboured most, he had drawn two long rows of Xs, for kisses. Ollie leaned against her, hugged her from behind, then wriggled into her lap.

'Why do you let him use you like a climbing frame?' Rebecca's mother had asked her. Rebecca was taken aback – it had never occurred to her that he shouldn't.

After a pause, she told me, 'Ollie was always touching me. He couldn't bear it if I was out of his sight. If I was on the phone or speaking to someone else, he used to do this thing to get my attention, he'd pat my waist and say, "Mummy, Mummy, Mummy" over and over—'

At once, we both heard those words – 'he'd pat my waist' – and remembered her dream: 'he patted my waist . . . he wanted me'. And we both realised that the dream wasn't about an old boyfriend. 'My dream is about Ollie and me, isn't it?' she asked.

Neither of us spoke.

'I miss him being my baby,' she said.

Rebecca longed for something impossible: a time when she was held, climbed on, kissed, nuzzled, loved by her three-year-old boy. She longed for Oliver's insistent demands on her attention – *Mummy, Mummy, Mummy* – to feel his hand touching her waist, and to feel that he needed her again.

On hate

Jessica B. began her Monday morning session by telling me about her weekend. She and her husband, Paul, had left their four-year-old daughter with her parents, then gone up to Cambridge to pitch for an architectural project. Paul suggested that they stay overnight, and their client, a university college, had organised for them to stay in an historic building. 'Medieval, timber-framed, with this fantastic original fireplace,' Jessica told me. 'It was perfectly cosy.'

The pitch had gone well and Paul wanted to celebrate. He prepared a romantic dinner for two and lit a fire. Jessica took a bath, then came out to find Paul in the cashmere jumper she had bought him for Christmas. 'He looked so cuddly.' They ate dinner and snuggled up in front of the fire. 'It was lovely. I know Paul wanted to have sex, but I just didn't feel like it. I wish I did, but I didn't. He didn't get annoyed with me – he's a real sweetie.'

Something in the way she said it – *sweetie* – grated on me. 'Can you hear the words you're using?' I said. '"Cuddly", "snuggle", "sweetie" – these are words we might use to describe a child, not a man who wants to have sex.'

'Sweetie *is* what I call Paul – do you want me to use other words?'

No, I told her, I wanted her to use her own words. But I thought her words suggested that she desexualised Paul.

Perhaps, she said. Last week, in the supermarket car park, she had seen a man she'd had a crush on at university. They didn't date, she didn't know him well, but there he was, helping two small kids out of a car. He was still athletic and tall; seeing him now with his children, Jessica found him even more attractive. Since that moment in the car park, she had imagined what it would be like to have an affair with him. She went silent.

Previously, she'd told me that Paul worked out and took care of himself – she thought he was still attractive, but she didn't feel attracted to him. I said, 'What I'm trying to understand is why Paul is now cuddly, a sweetie – and this man in the car park "athletic and tall".'

She couldn't explain. Jessica remembered collecting Paul from Heathrow several weeks earlier. He'd been away on a site visit for two days and she had missed him. In the taxi home she pulled him close and started to kiss him, but when he reciprocated her kiss, she heard herself tell Paul he should do up his seat belt. 'It's me,' Jessica said. 'I shut off.'

She remembered when they were first dating. A taxi ride from a West-End restaurant to Paul's flat – 'We couldn't keep our hands off each other.' But dating made her edgy. In some ways it was one of the most anxious periods in her life. There were days when she was convinced that Paul was looking to find someone sexier, more successful. Was he waiting for something better to turn up? She had hated the uncertainty.

As I listened, I thought about our first meeting. Jessica had been referred to me several months earlier by her doctor. He said she was overwhelmed balancing work and family, and taking care of her ageing parents. During that first meeting she told me that she didn't understand why her marriage had become so cold; she and Paul were barely having sex.

Her problem was common enough, and has been discussed by psychoanalysts for a hundred years. Freud described this predicament as second only to anxiety in causing misery to his patients. 'Where they love they do not desire and where they desire they cannot love,' he wrote. There are many reasons this dilemma can develop in a person, and many solutions. Jessica behaved like the patients Freud described, but after three months of psychoanalysis I didn't know why. Trying to talk with her about this seemed to have no effect. I felt I was getting nowhere.

Reluctant to repeat my ideas, or go over old ground, I was quiet until the end of her session, when she gathered her things and left.

Unusually, Jessica missed her session the next day. She left a telephone message saying that she wouldn't be in at all that week and that she'd explain when she next saw me.

The following Monday she arrived late. It turned out that she and Paul hadn't got the Cambridge job. She told me that the whole week had been so busy that she hadn't had time to think about it, or come to her sessions. She and Paul had been counting on the job financially. It was a big project for the firm. She felt their design was the best. 'I've just been so down,' she said.

'I'm struck that you didn't think of telephoning me when you felt so down.'

'I didn't know you needed me so much,' she said, and laughed. 'Weren't your other patients bringing you enough problems?'

Listening to Jessica, it occurred to me that she wanted to feel that she was the busy mother and I, along with her husband, was another demanding child. I told her this and reminded her of something she had told me early on with evident pride: her weight rarely changed; she could control her hunger. She had confided that it made her feel a bit high to not eat, especially when others were tucking in.

'That's just how I am,' she said. 'Do you want me to be like most people and comfort eat when I'm down?'

I told her that I was raising the question in light of our talking about sex last week – that I wondered if ignoring her sexual hunger helped her to feel a bit better, gave her a lift.

My question annoyed Jessica. She left, without saying goodbye.

The next day she returned and told me that, while there might be something in what I was saying, it didn't explain why she and Paul had stopped having sex.

I asked if she could remember what had happened – was there something specific that might have caused her to go off Paul?

It was after her daughter, Phoebe, was born, she said. 'That's natural, I suppose. I was completely sleep-deprived, leaking breast milk, and I felt that if I lost one more night's sleep I might go crazy. The last thing I wanted was sex.'

She remembered one particular night. Phoebe wasn't eating solids yet; she must have been just about six months old. Jessica was still breastfeeding. She was trying to get Phoebe on to a schedule, to sleep through the night. She had fed her at ten and put her down. Around midnight, Phoebe began to cry. Jessica thought she should just be rocked back to sleep. Paul rocked her for a long time, but Phoebe wouldn't be calmed. He was convinced that she needed more milk.

Jessica and Paul got into a terrible fight. She felt he wasn't supporting her in trying to get Phoebe on to a regular schedule, that he was undermining her. He said that if she didn't feed Phoebe he was going to get some expressed milk out of the freezer and do it himself, and he did. It turned out he was right – for some reason Phoebe was still hungry. 'I thought she could settle herself – self-soothe.'

The night got worse. Phoebe fell deeply asleep, they went back to bed, and Jessica began to cry. She expected Paul would put his arms around her, but he rolled over, turning his back. 'I asked him why he wouldn't cuddle me – and he said, "I thought you should self-soothe." I was awake all night, furious with both Phoebe and Paul. I hated them both.'

Jessica sighed. She told me that before she got pregnant, she had always imagined that she would know just what to do. She thought that she would be a good mum, certainly better than her own mother, better than most of her friends – and that having a baby would strengthen her relationship with Paul.

'You hoped having a baby would undo the unhappiness of your own childhood,' I said.

'I thought I'd find a kind of love with my baby that I'd never known before,' she said. 'A shared warmth, an understanding,' she replied. 'And I did – but I didn't know a tiny baby could also make me feel so angry.'

When Phoebe wouldn't sleep, or, once, when she bit another baby in the sandpit, Jessica found herself wildly angry. Phoebe's crying was particularly difficult – 'She howled, and every time she howled it was as if she was saying I was a terrible mother. I didn't do anything – I didn't grab or shake her, but I felt I could. It was awful.' Jessica shifted on the couch. 'I always thought I was a nice person,' she said, 'until I had a baby.'

At times when she felt bad about herself, she wanted Paul to support her, to reassure her that she was a good mother. When Paul's thinking differed from hers, she couldn't bear it. It felt like he was criticising her too. Looking back now, Jessica realised that she had always quickly recovered her affectionate feelings for Phoebe, but not for Paul.

I told her that she might be using Paul. If Paul was the problem, she could still think of herself as a good mum and Phoebe as a good baby.

Unexpectedly, Jessica sat up on the couch. She remembered something more. One day, in their kitchen, she was having tea with a friend, and Paul pulled a chair up to the table. As he did, Phoebe, who was sitting in Jessica's lap, reached out to grab at Jessica's mug, knocking it to the floor. It shattered. 'I shouted at Paul, called him an idiot. My friend burst out laughing. I really believed that the way Paul sat down had caused Phoebe to break my favourite mug.'

'Your first impulse was to blame Paul, hate him – so that you didn't hate Phoebe. It'll be hard to desire Paul if you're finding it useful to hate him.'

Raising her hands to her face, Jessica made a sound I didn't recognise at first. I'd never heard her cry.

At the end of the session, as Jessica stood to leave, I

remembered my impatience with the word 'sweetie'. 'Sweetie' wasn't a sign of intimacy or love – it was sugar-coated hate.

There is one more thing to add. A few weeks later, at work, Jessica saw Paul preparing for a client presentation with his assistant, a bright, pretty trainee architect. Jessica had never really noticed them together but now, watching from her desk, she saw them in the meeting room, the way they touched each other when they spoke, the way they both laughed at something he had said – and she really, really wanted him.

How lovesickness keeps us from love

Mary N., a forty-six-year-old housewife and mother of three, was admitted to hospital in a manic state. Just before her breakdown, Mary had attended a neighbour's garden party with her husband, and they'd met a man named Alan, a recently widowed barrister. At some point in the evening, Mary and Alan had struck up a conversation in the kitchen. They talked openly about his grief over his wife's death and hers over her sister's recent death from cancer. He proposed that she come to lunch at his house the following Friday. When Friday arrived, Mary showed up at his doorstep with a bouquet of peonies, a bottle of Sancerre, and a removal van containing all of her clothes and possessions, including some large pieces of furniture. Alan welcomed Mary and accepted her gifts – not until he saw the movers did he begin to grasp fully her intention. When he refused to let her inside, Mary became frantic, crying and tearing at her clothes. Alan called her husband, who in turn called the family doctor.

Four months after separating from his wife, Isaac D., a forty-one-year-old surgeon, attended a conference in America. Sitting in a bar at Kennedy Airport, he met a twenty-nine-year-old dentist named Anna. They chatted for about an hour and then went their separate ways. Arriving back in London, Isaac used the Internet to track her down. Two days later, carrying an armful of flowers and a pearl charm-necklace, he walked into her Buenos Aires dental practice. Straightaway, Anna called her father and her fiancé; they both came to the office and tried to get Isaac to leave. Only once the police had arrived and he was threatened with arrest did Isaac finally agree to go. One week later, sitting in my office, Isaac told me that he had always been prone to crushes, but this time was different, he had really fallen in love. He'd only agreed to come and see me because his doctor had insisted. He was prepared to discuss his feelings of rejection, but he couldn't see that there was anything wrong in his behaviour. 'I'm just an old-fashioned romantic,' he told me.

Most of us have come down with a case of lovesickness at one time or another, suffering its fever to a greater or lesser degree. In severe cases, lovesickness can lead to delusional behaviours (stalking, for example) or sexual obsession. When we are lovesick, we feel that our emotional boundaries, the walls between us and the object of our desire, have fallen away. We feel a weighty physical longing, an ache. We believe that we are in love.

Many psychoanalysts think that lovesickness is a form of regression, that in longing for intense closeness, we are like infants craving our mother's embrace. This is why we are most at risk when we are struggling with loss or despair, or when we are lonely and isolated – it is not uncommon to fall in love during the first term of university, for example. But are these feelings really love?

'I sometimes say – but not entirely seriously – that infatuation is the exciting bit at the beginning; real love is the boring bit that comes later,' the poet Wendy Cope once told me. 'People who are lovesick put off testing their fantasies against reality.' But given the anguish that lovesickness can cause – the loss of mental freedom, the dissatisfaction with one's self, and the awful ache – why do some of us put off facing reality for so long?

Often it's because facing reality means accepting loneliness. And while loneliness can be useful – motivating us to meet someone new, for example – a fear of loneliness can work like a trap, ensnaring us in heartsick feelings for a very long time. At its worst, lovesickness becomes a habit of mind, a way of thinking about the world that is not altogether dissimilar to paranoia.

Many years ago, I had a patient named Helen B., a thirty-seven-year-old freelance journalist. For nine years, Helen had been having an affair with a married colleague named Robert. Gripped by lovesickness, Helen was unable to think about him in a rational way. For years, Robert had broken his promises to her. He would suggest that they go on holiday together, and then take his wife instead. He had pledged to leave his marriage when his youngest child went to university – but that event had come and gone, and Robert hadn't made a move. Three months after Helen started her psychoanalysis, Robert told her that he had fallen in love with someone new and was leaving his wife for her. Helen did not reject or deny this information, but she seemed unable to grasp its implications. She told me that she could 'see through it' to 'what was really going on'.

'My friends always said "Robert will never leave his wife" but they were wrong – he is leaving her,' she told me triumphantly. Helen said that she was 'thrilled' – she believed that Robert's new girlfriend would 'never be able to handle him', so he'd eventually come back to her. This was a possibility, of course, but Helen seemed to believe it was a certainty, and refused to admit the obvious: Robert had fallen in love with someone else. Like the paranoid, the lovesick are keen information-gatherers, but one soon notices an unconscious intent in their observations – each new fact confirms their delusion.

For the first year of her psychoanalysis, I found that I could not help Helen to think differently. She reminded me of the conspiracy theorists who believe that Prince Philip murdered Princess Diana, or that the CIA planned the September 11th attacks – no amount of evidence could rattle her convictions. When I tried to point out that nothing Robert did seemed to alter her feelings towards him, she became irritated. 'Isn't that what *true* love is all about?'

When I teach psychotherapeutic technique, I often include Charles Dickens' *A Christmas Carol* on the reading list. I do this because I believe it's a story about an extraordinary psychological transformation, and that Dickens teaches us something essential about how people change.

In Dickens' tale, as you'll probably remember, the miserly Scrooge is visited by three ghosts. The ghost of Christmas past returns Scrooge to his childhood, to a series of unhappy moments: his father abandoning him at a boarding school, his young sister dying, his own choice to reject his fiancée in order to devote himself to moneymaking. The ghost of Christmas present shows Scrooge the big-heartedness of the poor Cratchit family, whose littlest member, Tiny Tim, is dying – a direct result of Scrooge's refusal to pay Bob Cratchit a decent wage. When the spirit of Christmas future shows Scrooge his own neglected grave, Scrooge is, at last, transformed.

Scrooge doesn't change because he's frightened – he changes because he's haunted. We can be frightened of gaining weight, but that alone probably won't cause us to change our diet. Haunting is different. It makes us feel – makes us alive to – some fact about the world, some piece of information, that we're trying to avoid.

What knowledge is Scrooge trying to avoid?

Scrooge doesn't want to think about the death of his mother, the death of his sister, or the loss of his fiancée – he cannot bear the thought that love ends. Dickens tells us that, before bed, Scrooge eats alone and reads his banker's book – his ledger of deposits, withdrawals and interest paid. I take this to mean that Scrooge spends his evenings comforting himself; as he reads his deposit book, he thinks to himself, 'You see? No losses, only gains.'

Ultimately, Scrooge changes because the ghosts unpick his delusion that you can live a life without loss. They undo his delusion by haunting Scrooge with the losses he has already experienced, the losses now being endured around him, and the inevitable loss of his own life and possessions.

Dickens' story teaches another lesson: Scrooge can't redo his past, nor can he be certain of the future. Waking on Christmas morning, thinking in a new way, he can change his present – change can only take place in the here and now. This is important because trying to change the past can leave us feeling helpless, depressed.

But Dickens' tale points to a further, darker and unexpected truth. Sometimes change comes not because we set out to fix ourselves, or repair our relation to the living; sometimes we change most when we repair our relation to the lost, the forgotten, the dead. As Scrooge grieves for those he had loved but put out of his mind, he begins to regain the world he had lost. He comes to life.

So if, inadvertently, a patient lets me know what haunts her – the thought she knows but refuses to think – my job is to be like one of Dickens' ghosts: to keep the patient at the scene, to let it do its work.

One Monday, during her second year of psychoanalysis, Helen told me that she had bumped into a newspaper editor she knew at an art gallery. For as long as Helen could remember, this editor, a woman in her fifties, had always looked impeccable – perfect hair and manicure; fresh, glowing skin. 'She has fabulous clothes and jewellery,' Helen told me. 'But then she can afford to spend a lot of time and money on herself because she doesn't have a family.' Helen had always admired this woman, but on this occasion, surrounded by younger people, the editor looked out of place, tired. As she was about to leave, Helen caught sight of the woman at the bar. 'She was too loud, trying too hard, standing too close to this young guy – it was embarrassing.'

I asked Helen if she wanted me to reassure her that she wouldn't end up like her editor.

'I'd die if I became like that – the thought of turning out that way? No husband? No family? Making a fool of myself at some trendy art show?' Helen paused for a few minutes. Then she changed the subject.

'I think you told me the story of your editor because you're frightened that you glimpsed your own future,' I said.

In the following months, from time to time, I would return

Helen to that evening at the gallery. The 'scene at the bar' became a kind of shorthand between us, representing Helen's denial of time passing, her desire to eternalise the present.

Many things brought about a change in Helen. But this image of what she might become was, I think, one of them. For as long as I'd known her, Helen had been troubled by the idea that since meeting Robert – almost ten years earlier – she'd become frozen in time. She was watching the lives of those around her transform – her friends were getting married, having children – while her own life was stuck in place. But her focus was always Robert. Attending a friend's wedding, she'd wonder, 'Why won't he commit? What's wrong with me?'

Then something began to change. One day, Helen described a friend's baby shower. The guests were all women, friends of hers from university. Instead of talking about whether or not she and Robert would ever have a baby, we talked about Helen's friends – their closeness, and their genuine concern for one another. She could see that their intimacy had deepened and would continue to do so.

One night, a little while later, during a dinner with this same group, she saw herself through their eyes – as a woman passionately involved with someone who was not real and disengaged from the people who actually cared about her. She'd often thought that her fantasies of Robert might be keeping her from a husband and baby, but for the first time she realised that they were keeping her from the love of her friends. 'I felt sick with sadness thinking about what I'd lost,' she told me afterwards. During dessert, her mobile rang; she saw that it was Robert, and she didn't answer. She turned back to be with her friends.

Changing

How a fear of loss can cause us to lose everything

When the first plane hit the north tower of the World Trade Center, Marissa Panigrosso was on the ninety-eighth floor of the south tower, talking to two of her co-workers. She felt the explosion as much as heard it. A blast of hot air hit her face, as if an oven door had just been opened. A wave of anxiety swept through the office. Marissa Panigrosso didn't pause to turn off her computer, or even to pick up her purse. She walked to the nearest emergency exit and left the building.

The two women she was talking to – including the colleague who shared her cubicle – did not leave. 'I remember leaving and she just didn't follow,' Marissa said later in an interview on American National Public Radio. 'I saw her on the phone. And the other woman – it was the same thing. She was diagonally across from me and she was talking on the phone and she didn't want to leave.'

In fact, many people in Marissa Panigrosso's office ignored

the fire alarm, and also what they saw happening 131 feet away in the north tower. Some of them went into a meeting. A friend of Marissa's, a woman named Tamitha Freeman, turned back after walking down several flights of stairs. 'Tamitha says, "I have to go back for my baby pictures," and then she never made it out.' The two women who stayed behind on the telephones, and the people who went into the meeting, also lost their lives.

In Marissa Panigrosso's office, as in many of the other offices in the World Trade Center, people did not panic or rush to leave. 'That struck me as very odd,' Marissa said. 'I said to my friend, "Why is everyone standing around?"'

What struck Marissa Panigrosso as odd is, in fact, the rule. Research has shown that, when a fire alarm rings, people do not act immediately. They talk to each other, and they try to work out what is going on. They stand around.

This should be obvious to anyone who has ever taken part in a fire drill. Instead of leaving a building, we wait. We wait for more clues – the smell of smoke, or advice from someone we trust. But there is also evidence that, even with more information, many of us still won't make a move. In 1985, fifty-six people were killed when fire broke out in the stands of the Valley Parade football stadium in Bradford. Close examination of television footage later showed that fans did not react immediately and continued to watch both the fire and the game, failing to move towards the exits. And research has shown, again and again, that when we do move, we follow old habits. We don't trust emergency exits. We almost always try to exit a room through the same door we entered. Forensic reconstruction after a famous restaurant fire in the Beverly Hills Supper Club in Kentucky confirmed that many of the victims sought to pay before leaving, and so died in a queue.

After twenty-five years as a psychoanalyst, I can't say that this surprises me. We resist change. Committing ourselves to a small change, even one that is unmistakably in our best interest, is often more frightening than ignoring a dangerous situation.

We are vehemently faithful to our own view of the world, our story. We want to know what new story we're stepping into before we exit the old one. We don't want an exit if we don't know exactly where it is going to take us, even – or perhaps especially – in an emergency. This is so, I hasten to add, whether we are patients or psychoanalysts.

I have thought of Marissa Panigrosso countless times since I first heard her story. I find myself imagining her in her office. I see her computer screen, the large windows. I smell the morning smells of perfume and coffee, and then – the first crash. I see her walk to the emergency exit and leave. I see her colleagues standing around. Tamitha Freeman leaves, and then a few minutes later returns for her baby pictures. I see myself there – in the south tower – and I wonder, what would I have done?

I want to believe that I would have left with Marissa Panigrosso, but I'm not so sure. I might have thought 'the worst is over'. Or worried that it would feel ridiculous to return the next day only to discover that everyone else had continued working. Maybe someone has told me, 'Hey, don't go. The plane hit the north tower – the south tower must be the safest place in New York' – and I stay.

We hesitate, in the face of change, because change is loss. But if we don't accept *some* loss – for Tamitha, the loss of her baby photos – we can lose everything.

Consider Mark A., a thirty-four-year-old who has just discovered a lump on his testicle but doesn't want to see his physician until after his holiday in Greece. Rather than attend the doctor's appointment his wife has made for him, he runs some errands, picking up suntan lotion and some T-shirts for the kids at Baby Gap. 'I'm sure it's nothing,' he says. 'I'll see to it when we get back.' Or there is Juliet B., a thirty-six-year-old who has been engaged for seven years to a man who regularly has affairs and visits prostitutes, and who behaves like a 'bully' with his clients and co-workers. 'I can't leave him,' she says. 'Where would I go? What would I do?'

For Mark A. and Juliet B. the fire alarm is ringing. Both are anxious about their situations. Both want change. If not, why tell a psychoanalyst? But they are standing around, waiting – for what?

How negativity prevents our surrender to love

Sarah L. is supposed to go away with her boyfriend for the weekend but, at the last minute, she decides to stay in with her girlfriends and watch television. Surprised, they encourage her to think again. 'You had a fantastic time going away with Alex before,' they tell her. But Sarah can't be swayed. 'I just don't feel like it,' she says.

Attractive, quick-witted and successful, Sarah began psychoanalysis because she felt stuck – at thirty-five, she was ready for marriage and hoping to start a family. Over the past few years, she has met a few men whom she considered 'promising', but none of her relationships has lasted. She can't say precisely what it is, but she senses that she might be doing something to spoil her chances.

'Why didn't you go?' I ask her. 'He's too keen,' she tells me, without conviction. 'I can only tell you what I told him – "I'd prefer not to."'

Sarah's phrase startles me – it's familiar, but I can't think where it comes from. Then I remember. It's the catchphrase of a character from literature: Bartleby the scrivener, the titular character of Herman Melville's short story, first published in 1853. Melville's protagonist is so odd that it's hard to know exactly what Melville wanted readers to make of him.

The story is narrated by a lawyer, who takes into his Wall Street practice a scrivener, or legal copyist, named Bartleby. Bartleby works at a small desk hidden behind a screen, his only window looking out on to a brick wall. Increasingly, Bartleby responds to the lawyer's quite reasonable requests with the words 'I would prefer not to,' eventually refusing to do anything at all. While the other employees work, eat and drink, Bartleby mutely stares out of his window. He never leaves the office and his presence becomes so impossible that the lawyer is forced to move his practice elsewhere. When the new tenants of his old offices cannot get rid of the haunting Bartleby, the lawyer returns and tries again to help him:

'"Bartleby," said I, in the kindest tone I could assume under such exciting circumstances, "will you go home with me now – not to my office, but my dwelling – and remain there till we can conclude upon some convenient arrangement for you at our leisure? Come, let us start now, right away."

'"No: at present I would prefer not to make any change at all."'

Agitated, the lawyer flees. The police remove Bartleby to

the Halls of Justice, better known as the Tombs. When the lawyer visits, Bartleby refuses to speak to him or to respond to the lawyer's pleas that he eat something. Returning several days later, the lawyer finds Bartleby, curled up, facing the base of the prison wall, dead.

Negativity – this 'I would prefer not to' state of mind – is our desire to turn away from the world, repudiating normal hungers. Repeatedly, Bartleby turns away to face the 'brick wall', 'dead wall', 'blank wall', 'prison wall' – the subtitle of 'Bartleby, the Scrivener' is 'A Story of Wall Street'. He is surrounded by food – Melville has even named his three co-workers Turkey, Ginger Nut and Nippers (lobster claws) – but he refuses to eat, ultimately dying of self-starvation.

The lawyer makes several attempts to coax Bartleby out of his withdrawal, but helping, it turns out, is not so easy. In fact, the story hints at a dark truth: it is the lawyer's help that causes Bartleby's situation to worsen.

I read 'Bartleby, the Scrivener' as a portrayal of the continuous struggle at the core of our inner world. In each of us there is a lawyer and a Bartleby. We all have a cheering voice that says 'let us start now, right away' and an opposing, negative voice that responds, 'I would prefer not to.' When we are in the grip of negativity, we lose our appetite for human connection. We become Bartleby and turn those close to us into lawyers. Unconsciously, we drag others into pleading our case to us.

As an example of this, consider the teenage anorexic and her mother. In the girl's refusal of food you will hear Bartleby; in her mother's nervous pleading you will hear the lawyer. Like Bartleby, the anorexic seems to feel no anxiety about her worsening situation. Her anxiety – which is her motivation for change – has found its way into her mother. We may be hearing two people speak, but it is not a dialogue they're having – the daughter's internal conflict is being voiced by two different people. In my experience, if this situation persists, if the two continue to act out Bartleby and the lawyer, they will arrive at a similar outcome.

When Sarah told me she had decided not to go away with Alex, I too was tempted to try to persuade her. Like everyone else, psychoanalysts do get caught in the lawyer's role; our job is to try instead to find a useful question. Our weapon against negativity is not persuasion, it's understanding. Why this refusal? Why now? Alex had done nothing particularly wrong; in fact, over the time Sarah had spent getting to know him, Alex had proved to be thoughtful and trustworthy. The change was in her.

Consciously, Sarah wanted to meet someone and fall in love, but unconsciously, there was another story. At this deeper level, love meant losing herself, her work, her friends; it meant being emptied out, neglected and possessed. Gradually, by recollecting some of her painful early losses, as well as the deep despair she suffered at the end of her first loving relationship, we began to make sense of Sarah's demurrals. Sarah was involuntarily negative because emotional surrender and attachment represented a loss, not a gain. Sarah's negativity was a reaction to her positive, affectionate feelings for Alex – it was a reaction to the prospect of love.

On losing a wallet

Recently Daniel K. began his session by telling me this story.

He'd been at home the previous afternoon when his office manager rang with good news – he'd won a major architectural competition to design a museum of culture in Chengdu, China. As the youngest and least-known architect on the shortlist, Daniel had not expected to win. 'We're going to have a lot of fun and we're going to make a lot of money,' his manager told him. Daniel was elated – this was, he felt, the breakthrough he and his small firm had been waiting for – and he immediately arranged with his wife to celebrate at a restaurant in the West End.

He decided to take the Tube. 'After I sat down, I took out my wallet and put my ticket inside. Then – and this is the thing I don't understand – I put my wallet on the seat next to me. I had the thought, "It's not smart to put it there. If you put it there, you'll lose it." At the first stop I realised I had taken the wrong train and I leaped off. As the doors closed I remembered my wallet. But it was too late – I'd left it on the seat. I ran to the nearest guard, he rang ahead and someone checked the carriage at the next station but my wallet was gone. I felt terrible – really terrible.'

Daniel paused. 'I cancelled my credit cards and dashed to the restaurant. I was late and of course my wife had to pay. Losing my wallet killed my mood – I felt awful. And I felt I'd done all this to myself – but why?'

He went on. 'As we were leaving the restaurant I got a text message: "I've got your wallet. Give me a ring so I can get it back to you." You'd think I'd be relieved, right? My wallet is found; everything is OK. But I didn't feel relieved at all. Actually, I think I felt worse. I was really down. I felt I'd squandered the pleasure of winning the competition.

'And then, outside the restaurant, I did another crazy thing. As soon as I finished reading the text message, I caught myself checking my pockets again to see if I could find my wallet. I *knew* someone else had it, and yet I couldn't stop myself looking for it.'

As I listened to Daniel, what struck me – and perhaps it strikes you too – is the way that loss followed loss. He loses his wallet, but only after getting lost himself (taking the wrong train). He loses his usual good sense (putting his wallet on the seat, not in his pocket). He loses the evening (the occasion of treating his wife) and then, after his wallet is found, he loses the fact of its recovery and finds himself searching for it in his pockets. But my patient's biggest loss was emotional – over the course of all this, he lost the sense of happiness that should have accompanied his success. Within hours, he went from being a winner to feeling like a loser.

'Success has ruined many a man', Benjamin Franklin once said. This is true enough, but what Franklin didn't mention is that we often work the ruin upon ourselves.

The American novelist William Styron lived this problem. In his memoir, *Darkness Visible*, he describes arriving in Paris from New York to receive the prestigious Prix mondial Cino Del Duca, a prize given annually to a pre-eminent scientist or artist. Styron began to deteriorate four months before the award ceremony, just after being told he'd won the prize. 'Had I been able to foresee my state of mind as the date of the award approached, I would not have accepted at all,' he writes. His day of triumph turned into a nightmare – 'gloom crowding in on me, a sense of dread and alienation and, above all, stifling anxiety'.

Styron attended the award ceremony, but then abruptly announced to his benefactress, Madame Del Duca, that he'd decided to skip the formal banquet she'd planned to give afterwards in his honour – a part of the day's pageantry that had been announced months before – so that he could meet up with a friend. Then, stunned by her reaction and horrified at his own behaviour, he heard himself apologising to Madame's assistant. 'I'm sick,' he told her, 'I have *un problème psychi-atrique.*' In the end, Styron stayed for the banquet only to discover halfway through the meal that he had lost both the $25,000 cheque he'd just been awarded and his emotional equilibrium. Distracted by his inward pain, he was unable to eat or speak; Styron's success brought him to the edge of suicide.

To psychoanalysts, Styron's problem is not unfamiliar: there are many men and women who work hard to attain a goal, achieve success, and then suddenly, cataclysmically, fall apart. What are the unconscious forces that cause us to sabo-tage ourselves – sometimes in even the tiniest of ways – when we've achieved a success?

To begin with, we may be undone if we don't foresee that winning is also losing.

Three years ago, I had a patient named Adam R., a teacher, who became extremely agitated and then dangerously depressed after being appointed headmaster of a well-known school – a job he had always wanted, but one that would require him to move to another town. At our first meeting, he told me about his past – he had felt a similar anguish after the purchase of his first flat and then again after his wedding. 'I want to be headmaster,' he said, 'but I never imagined how I would feel about moving. My whole life is here.' Like many of us, Adam was utterly surprised by the loss that winning can entail.

But through our work together, Adam and I came to realise that it wasn't just the move that depressed him. Unconsciously, he believed that each of his achievements took something away from his father. 'I feel bad becoming headmaster just as my dad is retiring,' Adam told me. I pointed out that the one thing had nothing at all to do with the other. 'I can see that,' he replied, 'but it feels aggressive. For the first time, I'll be earning more than my dad.'

In Daniel's case, his first instinct, like mine, was to suspect that the loss of his wallet signified some similar drive to undo his own success. And he too worried about how his success would affect others. 'It made me queasy when my office manager said, "We're going to have a lot of fun and we're going to make a lot of money." I felt a bit of a fraud. Am I really better than the nine other architects on the shortlist? I don't think so, and they won't think so either,' he told me.

Daniel dreaded his colleagues' contempt. His evening of loss might have been a way back to experiencing himself once again as an outsider. It was a way of saying to his fellow architects: 'I'm not having fun and I've lost my money – there's nothing to envy here.' Being an also-ran wasn't what he wanted but it was familiar, and safer than being a winner.

But why had he continued to search for his wallet once he knew it had been found?

The project my patient had won would, of course, require him to spend a considerable amount of time in Chengdu, and he hated being away from home. The week he'd spent in China for his interview had been awful, he said. The hotel he'd stayed in was 'dark and depressing'. While he was there, he found he could sleep only if he kept a light on. As he spoke, I had the mental image of a small boy switching on a nightlight, not because he wants to be able to find his parents during the night, but because he fears his parents will forget him – lose him – in the dark.

'The Kaverns of Krock,' he said suddenly. He was referring to a Dr Seuss story that had terrified him as a small child. He recited a bit of it for me. '"And you're so, *so*, *So* lucky you're not a left sock, left behind by mistake in the Kaverns of Krock! Thank goodness for all of the things you are not! Thank goodness you're not something someone forgot."'

Could that small gesture – patting his pockets for a wallet he knows isn't there – have been a way of distracting himself from another, more worrying thought: that he is about to be lost himself? Searching for his wallet might have been a way of soothing that particular anxiety. Better to be in the position of having lost something than to be something someone forgot.

A change in the family

About twenty years ago, I had a patient named Emily. Emily was ten years old, and had been brought to the clinic where I worked by her parents because she'd begun having 'accidents'. She wet her bed at night and one day tried to flush a pair of dirty pants down a school toilet, causing it to overflow.

Emily was a middle child. She had an older brother, Grant, who was twelve, and a new baby brother. Before meeting Emily, I met with her parents to learn more about the family. They told me that Emily was something of a mystery to them. While Grant was a model student, Emily was not. Emily, her mother said, was 'not very bright and really clumsy – she's always making a mess at the table'. When I remarked that Emily showed above average intelligence on the clinic's testing and that her fine motor skills were normal, her parents looked at each other in surprise. 'We were expecting you to tell us that she was dyslexic or something,' Emily's father said. He leaned forward, 'We just want her to be happy. It doesn't matter if she doesn't do as well as her brother.' We agreed that I'd see Emily every morning before school, and we'd meet without her once a month.

A few days later, Emily's father and brother brought her to the clinic. Father and son were both immaculately dressed – her father in a business suit, her brother in a school blazer. Emily, on the other hand, was a mess – hair uncombed, nose runny. She sat swinging her legs, looking down into her lap.

During our first session, Emily drew a picture of her family. After she finished, I pointed out that she hadn't drawn her new baby brother, Zac. She picked up the marker again, adding Zac to the picture – but she drew him in such a way that Zac was bigger than her. I had the thought that she didn't mind Zac, but she minded not being the baby any more, and I told her this. She then told me that since the birth of her brother no one took the time to sit with her when she was in the bath. 'My mum used to put toothpaste on my brush for me, but she says I'm a big girl now and I have to do it myself.'

For the rest of that first session we talked about all the changes in Emily's life since Zac's birth – how Mummy stayed in bed with Zac in the morning, Daddy made breakfast and took her to school; how she had to read her own story at bedtime. As the session was drawing to a close, I was tempted to tell her that she might be wetting her bed and soiling herself because she wanted to be washed and changed like her baby brother. But I didn't. I felt my words might shame her and in any case she hadn't brought it up. We'd talk about it, I decided, when she raised the subject.

A month later, at my next meeting with her parents, they told me that Emily had stopped having 'accidents', it seemed to them, after her very first session. They were grateful but they thought it best to stop the therapy. I felt differently and told them that we hadn't understood why Emily was so chaotic or why she was doing so poorly at school. Her parents, however, were insistent, and Emily stopped coming to see me. Four days later, they called to ask if I would take Emily back. She'd started having 'accidents' again.

During her year of therapy, there were three occasions, each immediately after her parents told her that they thought therapy should stop, when Emily had an 'accident'. I don't think these accidents were deliberate, rather it seemed to me an involuntary reaction, Emily's way of trying to keep our conversation from ending.

After the third occasion, Emily came to her session and made a drawing. She began by sketching a tall old house. Like a doll's house, it was a cutaway, so that you could see into the rooms. Then she drew a lorry and a motorcycle pulling up in front of the house. The truck was full of soldiers. As she drew a swastika on the side of the lorry, she said, 'These are the Nazis.' She drew two figures. 'We're here, hiding in the attic, we're safe.'

In fact, we did meet in a small therapy room, at the very top of a Victorian house that was home to the Anna Freud Centre. Emily explained that her father had told her that Anna Freud and her father had fled the Nazis and come to live in England. She told me that she knew all about Anna Freud – they'd read bits of her book in school. She knew Anna Freud received a diary from her parents for her thirteenth birthday, and that she told her diary everything – her most personal thoughts and feelings – that her diary was her comfort, her support. As she spoke, Emily turned back to the first page of her drawing pad, and there, beneath where she'd written her name, she wrote 'Who would ever think that so much can go on in the soul of a young girl?' While writing she told me, 'Anna Freud wrote these words in her diary.'

For the next year, Emily and I met. While she drew pictures, we discussed her thoughts and feelings – about school, home and the world. I thought Emily's conflating of the stories of Anna Freud and Anne Frank said something about how she felt about our sessions, that her notebooks of drawings, the sessions themselves, were her diary – her comfort, her support.

At the end of that year, Emily's parents and I agreed that the therapy could come to an end: she was doing better in school, she seemed better in herself. But the most surprising change was something I couldn't see. Someone else had to show it to me.

Standing in the waiting room, a year after we'd first met and a few weeks before her therapy stopped, I watched Emily leave the clinic with her mother and brother. 'I like the way Emily has her hair now,' the receptionist said. I agreed. 'What do you think about what's happened to the rest of the family?' she asked. I told her that I wasn't sure I knew what she meant.

She pointed out to me that over the past year she'd noticed that, as Emily got better, the rest of her family had become more and more dishevelled, scruffy. 'It happens a lot here,' she continued, 'as the children get well, their families change too.'

The receptionist's observation made me rethink the case. My sense was that my work with Emily helped her get a clearer picture of herself – her abilities and what she was capable of – as distinct from her parents' low expectations of her. She was better able to resist the role that was unconsciously assigned to her. Now I realised that without knowing it, or consciously wishing it, Emily's parents had made her the problem so that they did not have to deal with problems of their own. When she changed her family had to change too.

One week before my final session with Emily, I had my last meeting with her parents. Towards the end of that meeting, they talked about themselves, things had become very difficult between them in recent months – did I think marital therapy would help?

Why we lurch from crisis to crisis

When Elizabeth M. first came to see me she was sixty-six years old and had recently lost her husband to pancreatic cancer.

She was very late to her first session because, shortly before leaving her house, she had cut her finger picking up a piece of broken glass. She'd been pushing the plunger on her cafetière when it slipped and shattered. 'The bleeding's stopped, but do you think I should go to my doctor?' she asked me.

When I saw her the next week, she told me that she had just lost her handbag, which contained her mobile, wallet and keys. 'Should I have *all* the locks replaced?' she wanted to know. The week after that, she accidentally spilled red wine on a friend's beige sofa, ruining it. She asked me, 'How can I make this right?' Week after week, month after month, Elizabeth began each session by recounting her latest misfortune and asking my advice.

We worked together, carefully considering her options, but I often felt less like a psychoanalyst than like a fireman coaxing kittens out of trees. During those early sessions, Elizabeth never reported a dream, or talked about her feelings – there wasn't time; there was always some new problem that required urgent attention. I would think to myself: 'What terrible luck!' or 'When she gets such-and-such sorted out, then her psycho-analysis will really begin.' After several months, it finally dawned on me that these disasters would never end – that this lurching from crisis to crisis was at the heart of her psychoanalysis. I would have to understand it, if I were to understand her.

After about six months, Elizabeth confided that the first thing she felt in the morning was 'a depressed, choking anxiety'. She woke frightened, sometimes shivering with fear, until she remembered a problem, some urgent situation that required her to get out of bed and face the day. There are various ways to circumvent depressed, anxious feelings. It's not uncommon, for example, to exploit sexual fantasies, or to use hypochon-driacal worries. Elizabeth employed her disasters to calm herself – they were her tranquilliser.

It's also not uncommon to use some large-scale calamity, or someone else's personal disaster – the newspapers are full of both – to distract oneself from one's own destructive impulses, and I soon noticed this tendency in Elizabeth. When Elizabeth told me that she'd completely forgotten her sister's birthday lunch – 'It was in my diary. I don't know what happened. It completely slipped my mind' – I suggested that she might be cross with her sister over a particular recent incident, when she felt her sister had snubbed her.

'So you're saying I forgot her birthday on purpose,' she said.

'I don't think it was *conscious* – but it would explain why you forgot. Tit for tat.'

'I don't know.' Elizabeth was quiet. Looking around the room, she said, 'I'm going to have to bring you some energy-saving bulbs. You really ought to start thinking more about global warming.'

In 1956, the psychoanalyst Donald Winnicott, in an essay on unconscious guilt, pointed out in passing that a melancholic patient may irrationally confess to starting some major disaster, one to which he has no connection whatsoever. 'The illness', he writes, 'is an attempt to do the impossible. The patient absurdly claims responsibility for general disaster, but in so doing avoids reaching his or her personal destructiveness.' In other words, sometimes we might try to assume responsibility for a major disaster in order to avoid responsibility for our own destructive behaviour.

I began to understand that Elizabeth's oft-repeated question 'How can I make this right?' concealed a calamity that she knew she could not make right.

In the last year of his life, Elizabeth's husband had known that he was dying. He'd become increasingly frightened and could not bear to be alone. The more he needed Elizabeth to stay with him at home, the more claustrophobic she'd felt. 'I had many offers of help – I didn't need to go out to the shops as often as I did. And obviously my friends would have understood if I'd cancelled a lunch now and again. But I didn't.'

She'd told herself that going out helped her to keep her equilibrium, that she was better able to take care of her husband if she gave herself these little breaks. But there were other changes in her feelings too: she found it more and more difficult to touch her husband, let alone have sex with him. Frightened of his death, reminded of her own mortality, and angry about being left to someday face her death on her own, Elizabeth found herself rejecting her husband in his final months.

After a year of analysis, Elizabeth started to talk to me about her husband's painful last months. For the first time, she remembered a dream: 'My husband is dead but he telephones me at home. I'm so relieved he's finally ringing me. I go to answer but the phone isn't where it usually is. I can hear it ringing but I can't find it. I pull the cushions off the sofa, and then I pull the books off the shelves, but I still can't find it. I'm in a frenzy. I try to pull up the floorboards with my bare hands, breaking my nails. When I wake up, I'm sobbing.'

As she told me the dream, Elizabeth cried. She'd cried often enough about some disaster that had befallen her, but this was the first time I'd heard her cry because she'd hurt someone who loved her, and whom she loved.

In the immediate aftermath of a major disaster, politicians and journalists typically declare: 'This changes everything.' Disasters can change quite a bit. Even an uninjured onlooker can be moved to a new empathy or a new fear. The political context we live in can, and has, changed. But we can sometimes exploit a disaster to block internal change. Like Elizabeth, we can take on a catastrophe to stop ourselves feeling and thinking – and to avoid responsibility for our own intimate acts of destruction.

On being boring

Graham C. was boring. One night, his girlfriend, an economist who worked in the City, told him so. They had just had a dinner party, during which she'd watched him, again and again, thoroughly bore the person he was talking to. 'Can't you *tell* when someone goes dead behind the eyes?' she asked. Then she broke up with him.

A few weeks later, the senior partner at Graham's law firm called Graham into his office. He told him that his work was fine, and that he appreciated the long hours he was putting in. But he warned Graham that the clients weren't taking to him. If Graham wanted to make partner, clients would need to feel a loyalty to him; they should want to call him with their problems. Graham saw the future he'd imagined for himself slipping away. Worried and depressed, he came to see me.

For the first few months of his analysis, Graham bored

me too. As our work progressed, I found his sessions increasingly deadening. Before each session, I'd have a coffee and splash cold water on my face, but this didn't really help: boredom isn't drowsiness. For me, it's a bodily reaction more akin to nausea. I felt fine in the sessions before and after Graham's, and yet more and more numbed during his hour. I wasn't entirely sure why. Graham listened to my ideas and responded with his own; he raised questions and sought clarification; he was appreciative of my work – he even reported improvement. And yet, it all felt hollow. We talked *about* him, but I rarely felt as if he talked *to* me.

There was another riddle: Graham's life should have interested me. His parents and grandparents worked in the film industry and Graham's own work as a lawyer involved a number of intricate and intriguing cases. His life *was* interesting but, for some reason, he could not make himself interesting to others.

Boredom can be a useful tool for a psychoanalyst. It can be a sign that the patient is avoiding a particular subject; that he or she is unable to talk directly about something intimate or embarrassing. Or it can mean that patient and psychoanalyst are stuck; the patient is returning again and again to some desire or grievance that the psychoanalyst is failing to tackle. A boring person might be feeling envious, and might kill a conversation – disrupting it or paralysing it – because he cannot bear to hear a helpful or compelling idea coming from someone else. Or the boring patient may be playing possum – just as there are beasts in the jungle that survive by playing dead, some people, when frightened, simply shut down. It's also true that psychoanalyst and patient will sometimes unconsciously collude to desiccate the atmosphere between them because they fear things becoming too emotionally disturbed, or too exciting. (Some years ago, I found that my sessions with an attractive young female patient were getting more and more lifeless. If I had to guess, I'd say that we were unconsciously avoiding any sort of charge between us.)

But I couldn't understand what was happening in Graham's sessions. It was true that he tended to avoid commitment and conflict. I never had the sense that he was fully committed to practising law, for example – I thought he might simply be trying to please his parents. He was close to his parents, and still spent most of his holidays with them. But when I tried to look at the lack of disagreement in his family, he laughed. 'So that's it?' he asked. 'I'm depressed because I can't get angry with my parents?'

One day, Graham told me that he'd gone for a drink with Richard, a colleague from work. They'd arranged to hang out for a couple of hours, but after forty-five minutes Richard had suddenly remembered an errand he had to run, and had left. I suspected that Graham was telling me the story because he knew that Richard had been bored. And so I asked him: 'Do you ever feel you're boring others?'

'I notice when people stop listening or look away, if that's what you're asking.'

'Did Richard look away?'

'He looked away, but he wasn't bored.'

'How do you know he wasn't bored?'

'Because I wasn't being boring.'

'So you ploughed on,' I said.

'I continued,' he replied.

I began to suspect that there was something aggressive in Graham's willingness to inflict boredom. After all, he admitted that he noticed when his listener stopped listening. So *why* did he continue?

Graham had once told me about Sundays at his parents' home. For as long as he could remember, his parents had hosted his grandparents and various friends for Sunday lunch. He confessed that he found the lunches excruciating. 'A room full of adults, all talking, laughing together – I don't remember them ever inviting a family with children my age.' I imagined the loneliness Graham might have felt. Perhaps he was recreating in his listeners a feeling he'd carried with him since those lunches – perhaps his dullness was a form of despair.

A few months into analysis, Graham remembered a dream. In the dream, he was standing outside the house he grew up in. He wanted to go inside but couldn't. As a rule, I would want to focus on the content of the dream, to spend some time unpacking it with him, trying to understand his associations. And Graham took a very long time recounting it to me. He described the house and its history, and then went into great detail about his feelings for the various rooms and their decor. During a session a few days later, he spent a very long time describing a relatively minor incident from his childhood. And it hit me that Graham was silencing me. He understood that I would consider dreams and memories important, that I would not interrupt him, and so he took his time, staying in those stories as long as possible.

Graham's being boring *was* aggressive – it was a way of controlling, and excluding, others: a way of being seen, but not seeing. It also served another purpose. Especially in the context of his psychoanalysis, it protected him from having to live in the present, from having to acknowledge what was happening in the room.

When I spoke to him about what was happening in his life, his response was to look back, avoiding how he felt or what he thought now. 'I was never there,' says Hamm in Beckett's *Endgame*, 'Absent always. It all happened without me.' Graham's long detours into the past were a haven from the present. Over and over, without knowing it, he was refusing to let the present matter.

On mourning the future

'Hi. This message is for Stephen Grosz. My name is Jennifer T. I got your name from Dr W. in San Francisco. That's where I'm from. I was just wondering if you have time, and if you're accepting new patients? Or if you might be able to help me find someone?'

Jennifer was ten minutes late for her appointment. She was sorry, something urgent had come up at school, and she'd had to speak to another teacher before leaving. After settling herself in the chair opposite me, she said that she wanted to see a psychotherapist because her father had recently died. Four months earlier, he'd stopped on the hard shoulder of a highway to help a young couple whose car had broken down in the middle lane. Standing by the side of the road, gesturing to the couple to stay put, he was hit by a pick-up truck as it swerved to avoid the stalled car. He died in the ambulance on the way to the hospital. He was sixty-two.

She said that she had been particularly close to her father. Her parents had divorced when she was a teenager, and her mom had remarried. She was an only child. Although her dad was in California, they emailed and spoke often. An early riser, she liked to telephone her dad when she was getting up and making the coffee, and he was tidying up, getting ready for bed. 'The thing I don't understand,' she said, 'is that I feel oddly calm. I'm just not as upset as I thought I'd be.'

She told me that she hadn't cried since the funeral. The other night, while watching a DVD with her partner, Dan, she'd begun to cry. 'He put his arm around me. He thought I was thinking about my dad – but I wasn't, I was crying because of the film. Actually, I remember thinking I had to tell my dad about the film. He'd really like it.

'I just feel we're between calls. He's away from his desk and can't email me right now. He's not home from work yet, he's on the beach – he can't get reception. I don't feel he's died. I still imagine him being there when Dan and I get married, when we have children.'

For a second, I thought I'd missed something. As I was about to ask her if she was getting married soon, she told me that the other thing she wanted to talk about was Dan.

He was thirty-eight, four years older than her – an economist. He worked in the financial sector. She never said banking; everyone hates bankers. Originally, their plan was to work in London for a year or two and travel – and then, when they were ready, have children. But they'd been living in London almost four years, and she'd wanted to have children for – well, a long time.

Dan wasn't opposed to having children, she said, he just didn't feel that now was the best time. There was another thing. 'Last week we went out for lunch, and there was a family next to us, with two young kids. Dan asked the waiter for a different table. He hates mess. I worry that he might not be a good father.'

I asked her if they had a plan to get married – had they set a date?

She explained that Dan really didn't like pressure. He couldn't see the point of marriage. 'He'd say, "I choose you every day, why do we have to get married?"'

Several times during their relationship she'd pushed for some commitment, some idea of where they were going. A year ago, he told her that he'd consider marriage but that she would need to sign a pre-nup. She was stunned, and the idea of it seemed to take the wind out of her sails. She told me that she'd stopped asking for what she wanted, and was trying to accept what she had.

'You don't think he'll make a good dad, do you?' she asked.

'What do you think?' I asked.

'He can change, can't he?'

'What makes you think he wants to change?' I asked.

She was silent for a moment. Then she said she'd suggested

to Dan that they see a couples counsellor, but he wouldn't commit to anything like that until things settled down at work. Lately he'd been travelling a lot for work.

I asked her if she missed him when he was away.

She used to, but recently she'd begun to imagine her life if they broke up.

'What did you imagine?' I asked.

'I worry about him. I imagined moving back to the States, and ringing him to make sure he's OK. He's a good guy, but still a boy in many ways. He needs looking after.'

I was silent.

'You think I'm treating him like he's my baby,' she said. 'Is that why I'm accepting things as they are, not pushing to have a child of my own?'

I didn't know yet, I said. I told her that I was struck by her lack of anger. That Dan had changed his mind, let her down about having children.

She told me that she just didn't feel angry. 'I know I should – my friends tell me they would – but I can't. It doesn't bother me, not the way I know it should.'

Neither of us spoke for a minute or so, and then I asked her to tell me more about herself. Where had she grown up? What was her mother like?

For the next half-hour or so, Jennifer told me many things about her family and childhood. Her mother and father both worked at various jobs in and around San Francisco. Her mom worked in a large department store and then opened her own clothing store. Sometimes there was money, at other times it all just seemed to disappear. When she was ten, they lived in a large Victorian house and then, suddenly, they moved into a two-bedroom condominium that smelled of acrylic carpeting.

She told me that her family didn't have a regular social life – her mom and dad didn't seem to have any friends, no one came to dinner. Twice a year, at Thanksgiving and Christmas, the leaf was put in the dining-room table, the white linen tablecloth was starched and ironed and they entertained her mom's family. She and her mom began preparing several days in advance, there was always too much to eat, and the conversation – what little there was – concerned the food.

Dan's family was from Boston. They weren't that wealthy, but they lived differently. His father was a doctor, his mom worked for the mayor's office. They had a big kitchen and there always seemed to be people around the table talking. His parents liked having parties. Jennifer loved staying there. She felt at home, looked after. When she and Dan were married, their home would be like that too. She imagined they'd live nearby – 'they'll be wonderful grandparents'.

As she spoke, I thought about the similarity between her situation with her father and her situation with Dan – her father had died, her relationship with Dan seemed dead. About both, she was, as she said, oddly calm, not bothered. Why wasn't she grieving her father's death, or the death of her relationship with Dan?

I tried to explain what I was thinking to Jennifer. 'It seems to me that you're so caught up in the future – your father being at your wedding, having a home near Dan's parents – that you don't feel upset about how your life is now, in the present.'

Looking at me, smiling, she nodded. I thought, she's agreeing with me the way she agrees with Dan – she doesn't get it, she isn't anxious for herself. 'You don't seem to be worried,' I said. 'You could get stuck here for a very, very long time.'

'So you're saying that Dan won't change,' she said.

I looked at the young woman opposite me. I imagined my own daughter, years from now, Jennifer's age, trapped in a lifeless relationship – what would I want a colleague to tell her? What could he say that might help?

I'd want her to be told that sometimes we have to mourn the future, that many young couples have more future than present. Breaking up means giving up not only their present, but the future they'd dreamed of. Leaving a relationship, starting a new life, meeting the right person, getting married and having a child can take a long time – much longer than she might imagine. She might have to go through some pain to have what she wants. But facing up to reality, however dreadful, is almost always better than the alternative. I'd want my colleague to tell my daughter that, should she so want, he'd try to help – he'd face all this with her.

I said all of this to Jennifer. She nodded again and said she felt upset by what I'd just said, but glad that I'd said it. She was still tearful as she left.

Psychoanalysts are fond of pointing out that the past is alive in the present. But the future is alive in the present too. The future is not some place we're going to, but an idea in our mind now. It is something we're creating, that in turn creates us. The future is a fantasy that shapes our present.

How anger can keep us
from sadness

Several years after qualifying as a psychoanalyst, I had a patient named Thomas. Thomas was nine years old and had just been expelled from school.

A few months before I first met him, the nurse at Thomas' school had found belt marks on his arms and legs. She also found bruises and nail marks on his upper arms – parallel injuries, indicating that he'd been grabbed and shaken. Thomas told the nurse that his mother had beaten him – and that he wanted to kill himself. Social services were called. Thomas' mother told a social worker that she was at her wits' end; that Thomas never listened to her; he was just impossible. She didn't know what to do. 'Everything would be OK,' she said, 'if only Thomas tried to be good.'

Thomas' teacher was asked by the local authority to prepare a report. She described him as 'distracted' and 'in his own world'. He wandered around the classroom during lessons, she wrote; he resisted eye contact, and he had begun describing violent fantasies to his teachers and classmates, easily and often.

Thomas told the social worker who met with his family that he wanted to kill his mother – 'Cut her open with a big knife, pull out all her intestines, then put her on a torture rack until all her joints snap.' Thomas told the assessing child psychiatrist that he wanted to murder a little girl in his class – 'I'd like to chop her head off,' he said. The next day Thomas brought a large kitchen knife to school – 'to show her'. He was immediately expelled, and enrolled instead in classes at the children's psychiatric unit where I was working.

Thomas was seen by a number of doctors – several children's psychiatrists, a psychotherapist, an educational psychologist and a paediatrician. All agreed that he was suffering from high-functioning autism, or Asperger's syndrome. One psychiatrist believed that Thomas might also be suffering from Tourette's syndrome or a pre-schizophrenic disorder; another described him as having 'manic and psychotic features'. The psychiatrist in charge of Thomas' treatment prescribed a course of medication and recommended that Thomas be offered analysis five times a week.

Thomas and I met in a small consulting room down the hall from the unit's classrooms. There was a sink and a cupboard with eight lockers, one locker for each child who was having treatment in that room. Thomas' locker was stocked with the standard supplies: paper and washable markers, string, tape, plasticine, a family of small cloth dolls, and several small plastic animals. The idea is that a child's play will be like an adult's free association, that these supplies can help a child to express the emotions they might not be able to put into words.

During his first session, Thomas told me that he wanted to kill one of his teachers, and then he told me that he wanted to kill me. I suspected he didn't mean what he was saying, that he was just trying to be disturbing. When I attempted to talk to him about what he was feeling, he responded by going to his locker and taking out his supplies. He ripped up the paper, tried to break the markers, stomped on the cloth dolls and then threw everything into the sink and turned on the tap. I told him that I thought he was trying to show me how angry he was and how tangled up and messy his feelings were. He asked to go to the loo. I waited just outside the door. I heard the toilet flush, water running in the sink, and then the sound of breaking glass. Thomas had smashed a small window above the sink with his right hand. His wrist was cut and gushing blood. He was shocked, and yet he cried out, 'I've been shot, I've been shot. I've been shot in the Middle East.'

It was difficult for me to get a handle on what had just happened. Thomas was shaken, but his reaction seemed like a performance.

We met the next day, and while Thomas was quieter, he

still seemed determined to unsettle me. He spent most of the session calling me 'big tits' and 'fat lesbian'– phrases, he told me, that upset his female teachers. The following week, he drew swastikas on the walls and furniture, goose-stepped his way around the room, and called me a dirty Jew. '*Sieg Heil, Sieg Heil,*' he shouted.

A few weeks later he began a series of drawings. These pictures, dashed off in a minute or two, showed him standing over me, a meat cleaver in his hand, chopping me into pieces. Some days, he'd then draw another scene: a picture of himself sitting at a table, a napkin around his neck, eating my body parts.

While these sessions were disturbing, I wasn't too caught up in his various attacks – they were extreme, yes, but somehow they never felt personal. And, little by little, Thomas was telling me about his life. After two months of treatment, his teachers reported that his behaviour in the classroom had improved – he was able to use the therapy room as a place to discharge his anger and confusion.

Then Thomas began to spit in my face. 'I don't make rude gestures, do I?' he'd say, just before giving me the finger. 'I'm not kicking the door, am I?' 'I'm not jumping on the couch, am I?' 'I'm not spitting on you, am I?'

One day, we were sitting at the low table in the therapy room, and Thomas told me that he missed his friends. He'd once seen Oliver – his best friend from school – at the supermarket, but Oliver wasn't allowed to talk to him any more. He sounded sad and I told him so. He immediately spat in my face, twice, then ran to the couch and began to jump up and down on it. I told him that my words – that he sounded sad – had upset him, and that he'd spat at me to get the hurt out of himself.

Throughout our sessions, I tried to describe his behaviour to him in words I thought he could understand and use – I told him that his spitting was a way of getting rid of me before I could get rid of him; a way of controlling the distance between us. I described his spitting as a confession of guilt, an attempt to provoke a punishment from me. Another time I told Thomas that I thought he wanted me to be enraged with him so he'd know for certain that he was the only person in my mind. These interpretations, and others, seemed to have little or no effect. For the next year and a half – in every session – Thomas spat in my face.

Although I was receiving weekly supervision and attending a regular clinical seminar of psychiatrists and psychoanalysts who worked with children – all of whom had been thoughtful and helpful about my sessions with Thomas – I'd reached a breaking point. I began to dread the anger I felt after each of his attacks. It wasn't just that I didn't feel I was getting anywhere, I was beginning to lose faith in what I was doing.

I rang a colleague, Dr S., who had practised child and adult psychoanalysis for over fifty years. One rainy evening I left my office in Hampstead and drove to Dr S.'s house across town. Settling in a chair across from her, I began to unpack my files.

'Set your notes aside,' she said. 'Just tell me about him.'

For the next half-hour, I told her Thomas' story. I tried to describe the atmosphere between us, what I felt was going on. She listened, and asked a number of questions about his birth and early childhood, his parents and younger sisters, his psychiatric diagnosis and school reports. Then she asked, 'How do you feel when he spits on you?'

'Angry,' I said. 'Despairing too – but mostly angry, and guilty about my anger.'

'There are a number of children at the unit who spit. Does it always affect you like this?'

'No,' I said. I described a six-year-old boy diagnosed with autism. A few weeks earlier, we'd been kicking a ball back and forth in the playground; he'd become overexcited and, running up to speak to me, had spat on me instead. 'He didn't make me feel angry. On the contrary, I wanted to reassure him that he hadn't done anything wrong – I wanted to put my arm around him.'

Dr S. was silent a moment. 'I'm wondering if you have an expectation that Thomas can control his spitting. Maybe he can, maybe he can't. But because you think he can control his spitting, you're angry when he doesn't. You might consider the idea that he needs you and others – his mother, his teachers – to have this expectation. He needs you to be angry with him.'

Dr S. was right. Calling me a fat lesbian, a dirty Jew, giving me the finger, kicking the door – how hard Thomas had worked to find something that would make me angry. It had taken three months, but eventually he'd found the thing that would disturb me – and then he'd done it over and over and over again.

'But why are we stuck here?' I asked her.

'Think about the impasse,' she said. 'You know that when there's a deadlock it's usually because the impasse serves some function for both the patient *and* the analyst. Think of this deadlock as an obstacle that the two of you have created. What purpose does it serve you?'

We carried our coffee cups into the kitchen. I thanked her, and left. On the drive home, I was haunted by her question.

The next day I collected Thomas from his classroom, and he ran ahead of me up the stairs to the therapy room, yelling, 'Broken, broken, broken!' When we reached the door, he turned and looked at me: 'Well, do you have anything to say about that?' Before I could answer, he spat in my face.

We went inside. 'When you spit on me,' I said, 'you want me to get angry with you, because if I'm angry with you, it means I believe you could be different than you are. If I'm angry, it means I still believe we can fix what's broken.'

He was silent for a moment, and then I asked him, 'Can you tell me what's broken?'

'My brain's broken, stupid.'

He walked over to the small chair I was sitting on. 'My brain doesn't work, not like other people's.'

Sitting down next to me at the low table, he described looking out of the bus window on his way to the unit that morning. Everywhere there were children in school uniforms, with book bags, gym kits and footballs. He recognised many of the boys and girls from his old school. They were growing up, doing new things. 'I don't have a book bag. I'm crap at football. I do baby stuff at school. Did I tell you that my sisters practise their multiplication tables on each other? They're younger than me but they can do all these things I can't do 'cos their brains work. Mine's wrecked.'

He looked me in the eye. 'It's really sad. Isn't that really, really sad?'

'Yes, it is really, really sad.'

There was a great stillness in the room.

Two days later, he spat at me once more, and then never again.

Looking back, it is clear now that Thomas and I were at an impasse because neither of us could bear the thought that he was irreparably damaged. And it was only when we were both able to be sad, to despair because we couldn't fix what was broken, that his spitting stopped serving a purpose for us and we were able to move forward.

Thomas is now a grown man. He lives in the countryside

with one of his sisters, and he has a job in the mailroom of a small company.

Several times a year, usually when his psychiatrist is away, he rings me. He begins by asking me if I remember when his psychoanalysis began. I say yes. And then he tells me the exact time, the day of the week, and the date, of our first session. Then he asks me if I remember when his psychoanalysis ended, and I say yes. And then he tells me the exact time, the day of the week, and the date, of our last session. He'll tell me that was a long time ago, 'but it was an important time'. Sometimes he tells me about something that has happened to him recently, but more often than not he wants to talk about something that happened to him when he was a boy. And then, just before hanging up, he always asks, 'Do you think about me, do you remember what we talked about?' And I always reply, 'Yes, I do.'

On being a patient

Tom rang to tell me he had an eleven o'clock meeting with a radio producer in my neighbourhood; we could have lunch afterwards. 'Why don't we go to the Italian place around the corner from you?' he asked.

Five years earlier, when he had felt himself sinking into a depression, Tom had asked me to recommend a psychoanalyst. I'd referred him to Dr A., a woman I'd trained with and whose work I admired. Tom and I had been friends for almost twenty years, and we saw each other often – at least once a week. But during these past five years, he'd never mentioned his analysis, and, out of respect for his privacy, neither had I.

We met for lunch and talked about his upcoming radio series. By the time the waiter cleared our plates and brought coffee, the lunch crowd had gone; the place had emptied out.

Tom turned towards me. 'You didn't exactly lie to me,' he said, 'but you didn't tell me what to expect.'

'I'm not sure I know what you mean,' I said.

'Analysis. For the longest time, I just couldn't understand what was happening in my analysis. Dr A. was so focused on . . .' He trailed off.

'On what you were thinking?' I asked.

'Not even on what I was thinking – that seemed to be the whole point. She spent so much time on all this minutiae, on things that seemed to have nothing to do with what I was thinking.'

'I don't understand,' I said.

'I'm sure you do, but I'll give you an example.' Tom studied his cup for a moment. 'I get to her office. I ring the bell. She's got a buzzer system. What am I supposed to do if she doesn't release the door straight away? Should I ring the bell again? If I ring again, will she think I'm annoying? Then she releases the door. Her office is on the fourth floor. I have to take the lift. I'd like to take the stairs, but if I walk up, I'll be sweaty. So I take the lift.

'But the lift is a bit of a problem. I wouldn't want anyone to see that I'm going to a psychoanalyst – I'm antsy about that. So I get to the fourth floor and make it to her door. On the door she has one of those push-button combination locks, so that patients can let themselves into the waiting room. Sometimes I fumble with the lock and I get the combination wrong. Is she listening? Is she thinking, "What a klutz?"

'I'm in the waiting room five minutes early. Should I start

reading something? She once told me that it was interesting that I had started to read something despite the fact that I had only a couple of minutes before the start of my session. Maybe I shouldn't read. What do I do if someone else comes into the waiting room? Do I smile? What do I do if I see her colleague – do I say hello to him? Is there a rule about this stuff?

'She's one minute late coming to the waiting room to get me. Now it's two minutes. Has she forgotten me? She comes into the waiting room. Do I look at her, or not look at her? As I follow her into her consulting room, do I look around the room, or not look around the room? What do I want to see? Am I trying to avoid seeing something?

'Now I'm at the couch. Do I really lie down and put my wet, dirty shoes on her nice clean couch, or do I take them off? Do patients normally take off their shoes or not? I don't know. If I do take my shoes off and most people don't, I look peculiar. But if I don't take my shoes off and most people do – then I'm dirty. I decide that I'd rather be peculiar than dirty. So off come the shoes.

'By the time I finally lie down on the couch, I've been through all of that. This entire discussion – my sense of being reproached and my sense of self-reproach, this whole saga of doubt and trouble – all of it has been conducted before either of us says a word.'

Tom downed his espresso.

'It took a long, long time – probably a couple of years – to really divulge all that toing and froing clearly because, frankly, who wants to let someone else know just how absolutely small your own preoccupations are? But Dr A. kept returning to this sort of stuff, kept encouraging me to talk about it. We spent weeks on that shoe thing, for God's sake. I wasn't expecting that.'

'What *were* you expecting?'

'I thought I was going to lie on her couch, and reach into the past, and then we'd discover some buried trauma that she'd elegantly unpack for me . . . Or we'd discuss my Oedipus complex, or a dream about my dad's dick. Of course, eventually we *did* talk about my family and my past – she made those connections – but what surprised me was the amount of time she spent building up this picture of what was going on in my head. Hour by hour, day by day, week by week, she tuned in to the way I think. It wasn't what I imagined.

'Slowly, it emerged that at any point in that journey from her front door to the couch, I felt I might be scolded. If I didn't think that somebody was about to criticise me then this stuff shouldn't be a problem, right? I just ring the bell another time, so what? I fumble with the door, so what? I put my shoes on her couch, big deal.

'It turns out that a lot of the stuff I did – like taking my shoes off – I did because I didn't want to give her any excuse to tell me off. I had in my head the idea that she was someone who would come down really hard on me if I got her couch dirty. Who was this person who was going to be so cross with me? Was it my parents? Was it me? It certainly wasn't her. She couldn't care less if I kept my shoes on.

'And then it became clear – painfully clear – that I'm not just like this when I go to see my psychoanalyst. My everyday rules of engagement are so frustrating and weird. If someone doesn't immediately respond to an email I've sent, I feel criticised. If their response is a little cool, I'm at fault. Most closings – "kind regards", "best wishes" – feel like a rejection.

'I take almost everything personally. I get on the Tube: I get a seat – victory; I don't get a seat – defeat. I get a parking place – victory. I don't get the parking place – defeat. The repair man can come over straightaway – victory. I've left a fleck of shit in the toilet – defeat. These tiny, tiny moments are the way I measure my progress in the struggle that is daily life. Moment to moment, my thinking is utterly, unremittingly banal.'

'But it's not banal,' I said.

'No, you're right. It's not, because, of course, there's a pattern to these petty thoughts. I was operating on the assumption that people were basically reproachful. And because that was built into the way I did almost everything, I felt caged. All these moments weren't just the way I thought about my life – they *were* my life.'

Tom looked at his cup. 'Do you want another coffee?'

I nodded.

We called the waiter over, and ordered two more. Then Tom went on. 'Bit by bit, it became clear that this wasn't just about reproach, it was about something bigger. I thought my life was structured around a desire to live well. But I found that what I really wanted was to be clean. It's all there in that business about putting my shoes on the couch. Obviously, to anyone else, this will seem crazy, but I was beginning to see something that made sense to me.

'It turned out that there was no grand trauma behind my feelings of depression and isolation. What there was, was my incessant scrutinising, my calibrating myself to fit in with others. In analysis, my first impulse was the question: what does Dr A. want? That shoe nonsense was my attempt to fit in with what she wanted. But who knows what other people want? All of our thinking about other people's desires is assumption – assumption, assumption, assumption.

'I'd like to think I'm pretty astute,' Tom said. 'The truth is, sometimes I'm right, sometimes I'm wrong. The real question is whether or not we're trapped by our assumptions. I wasn't aware that I felt people were fundamentally fault-finding. I didn't know that my idea of a person is of someone who wants to scold me. I just thought people *were* that way, but it turns out I was wrong.'

Tom leaned back in his chair and said: 'Dr A. had another insight which I didn't see coming. It isn't always true, but it was in my case, that if you're frightened of being criticised, you're probably pretty critical. And what a surprise – it turns out that I'm a critical person. It turns out that when I'm not finding fault with myself, I keep busy reproaching others. I won't bore you with the one thousand and one things that are wrong with the decor in Dr A.'s office – or with Dr A. herself. You can imagine.'

Tom leaned forward and put his hands on the table. 'Do you know the word captious?'

I shook my head.

'I didn't either. Fabulous word – it means apt to notice and make much of trivial faults. Fault-finding. Difficult to please. Sound like anyone you know?' He set down his cup. 'I must have been an analyst's nightmare.'

I stopped him. 'Hardly,' I said. 'It sounds to me like you did exactly what you were supposed to do. You went in and told her what you felt. I don't think it was too difficult for her to spend an hour a day with you.'

'Thanks,' he said, 'but that's bullshit.'

'No, it's not.' I said. 'A nightmare is the patient who doesn't tell you what's on his mind. He drinks, secretly. He slaps his child, but he can't – or doesn't – tell you about it.'

'Not telling isn't my problem,' Tom said.

'No, you're an honest guy.'

'I didn't want my analysis to fail.'

'But some people do. Think of the teenage boy who is about

to be thrown out of school. Week after week, session after session, he sits silently for the whole hour. The analyst does the right things, makes thoughtful and true interpretations to the boy about why he won't speak to her. But, still, he won't engage. It may be that the boy needs the therapist to fail in order to feel that someone else is more useless than he is.'

Tom nodded. 'That's not me. But I really could be very negative,' he said.

'She's trained to think about your negativity, and she did. But OK, imagine your problem pushed a little bit further – an intensely negative patient. Imagine a patient who is so thin-skinned that he experiences almost every one of his psycho-analyst's comments, no matter how true, no matter how gently phrased, as if it were an attack. Even the analyst's silence feels like a reproach. Or maybe he continually scans the room to find the things that the analyst cares about – cut flowers, pictures on the wall, books – and day after day he mocks them. That's a difficult patient.'

'What do you do when you have a patient like that?'

'I might see them first thing in the morning.'

'No, seriously.'

'Seriously. I advise my students not to see too many patients like this, and to see them first thing in the morning, when they're less likely to get irritated.'

'But isn't it impossible not to take things personally?' Tom asked.

'Sure. I get irritated, but hopefully I'll find the reason the patient needs me to be irritated. My job is to listen, then check what I'm hearing against my emotional reactions – like with the teenage boy. He made his analyst feel angry and like a failure; she understood that he needed her to fail.'

Tom nodded.

I said: 'You brought in your criticisms of Dr A., and she thought about them with you. What can really be worrying is when a patient needs to think too highly of his analyst and the analyst goes along with it. Analysts have anxieties too – usually about their capacity to handle what the patient brings to them. Almost every analyst has, at one time or another, colluded with a patient to keep that patient's most disturbed feelings – anger or madness – from entering the room. It doesn't sound like that happened very often with Dr A.'

We were quiet for a minute.

Then I said: 'I can't figure out from what you're telling me – did your analysis help?'

'Dr A. and I are discussing this very question in my sessions right now, because I think it's time to stop. If you're asking me if I'm fundamentally different – I don't know. I can't tell. I think I'm fundamentally less critical of myself. I do know that I'm more aware.'

'That the way you were thinking trapped you?' I asked.

'I'm more aware of what's going on behind the scenes,' Tom told me. 'And that gives me a degree of choice. When I find myself feeling hurt or depressed, I can try to decode the feeling – I can decide if it's something I'm doing to myself or something that's being done to me. This gives me a way out.

'When you have no choice, you're doomed, you're stuck in a web of reproach and self-reproach. You have this way of thinking – a way of being – so deep in you that you can't question it, you can't even know it. You just live it. Having a choice is a very, very big liberation.'

Tom watched the waiter crossing to the front of the restaurant. 'I've got to tell you this,' he said. 'A couple of weeks ago, I was lying in bed. Jane was downstairs making us a pot of tea. I could hear the boys in their bedroom, laughing, playing with their light sabres – a perfect Saturday morning. I reach over and switch on Radio 3. Some piece of music ends and then the announcer says, "In place of our scheduled programme we're going to broadcast a programme by the historian and presenter" – and at this point I'm thinking "Oh fuck, for fuck's sake," – and the announcer continues with his big, fat introduction for this marvellous, world-conquering genius. And I'm thinking "Oh for fuck's sake, who is your fucking expert?" And, just as I'm about to switch off the radio, he says my name. They were rebroadcasting a programme I did a few years ago. I burst out laughing. It was such a surreal moment.

'Who knows why they were repeating an old programme of mine? I presume the CD they were going to play was scratched. Who cares? The thing is – I'm still pricked by all the real and surreal stuff life throws at me. I still want to be the only expert in my field, and there's still part of me that wants to believe that if I stay nice and clean, and work really hard, and I'm a big success, I'll be protected from depression and anxiety.

'What's different now is that I have in my memory this repertoire of exchanges with my analyst to call on, that I can use to understand my way out of a painful moment. I feel less lonely now.'

The waiter put the bill down between us. 'Let me get it – you paid last time,' Tom said.

I still wondered why we hadn't talked about his analysis before, and I asked him.

'I couldn't talk about my analysis because I didn't know how to talk about it. How could I tell anyone – including you – about that shoe malarkey without them thinking I was wasting my time and money? I wasn't sure anyone would see the bigger thing.'

Buttoning our coats, we stepped outside. Tom put his arm around me and gave me a hug. I hugged him back.

We stood for a moment on the pavement. Tom motioned up the hill towards the post office and shops. 'You going up or down?' he asked.

'Down, back to the office.'

I watched Tom walk up the hill, to take the Tube home. As I stood there, I found myself filled with a recognisable feeling, a disquiet that sometimes comes over me after a patient has left my consulting room, and I'm left with the sense that we've only talked *around* what's truly at the heart of the session. I feel that I've failed both my patient and myself, and I want to redo the previous hour, start again the session just ended. Of course, Tom wasn't my patient, and this wasn't a session. We were two old friends having lunch. But it bothered me that neither Tom nor I had talked directly about what he'd called 'the bigger thing' – neither of us had used the word love.

As I lost sight of him, I was still thinking about our conversation. Tom's minutiae – the smell of his sweat, the mud on his shoes; how opposite this view of himself from my own picture of this big, gentle, civilised man. I thought about his fear that if he was known, if he was seen as he believes he truly is, he would be found dirty, broken. And being dirty and broken – how could he love, or be loved?

Going back

As a gift to my father for his eightieth birthday, my wife and I organised a trip to Hungary. We would travel from Budapest to the Carpathian Mountains, taking in all the landmarks of my father's childhood: the house he was born in, his grammar school, his grandparents' farm and the surrounding countryside.

Through a genealogy website I made contact with a man named Alex Dunai, a tour guide from Lvov, a city in the Ukraine, who had established a reputation for tracing long-forgotten villages. Part detective, part translator, Alex often worked with the children of people who were dislocated by the Second World War. As my wife and I tried to find the places my father remembered on a modern map – the names had been changed as national boundaries shifted – Alex and I emailed back and forth, designing our itinerary. Based on the little my father had told me about the village where he grew up, Alex and I agreed that it was probably best to begin our trip in Mukachevo.

We arrived at the Hotel Langer in Mukachevo one afternoon in late May. Mukachevo is now a part of the Ukraine, about two hundred miles from Budapest. The air was hot and dusty, a vendor on a corner near the hotel was selling strings of dried mushrooms and yellow cherries. Though the streets were crowded, we seemed to be the hotel's only guests.

My father suggested we put our suitcases in our rooms and go for a walk. We followed him, first to the town centre, and then down a series of side streets. He moved swiftly, without speaking. Sensing his familiarity with the place, I let him lead us wherever he wanted. As we waited to cross a street, my father told us that from the age of fourteen to eighteen, he had boarded during the week here, in Mukachevo, with a widow, a woman named Anna Treichman, so that he could attend school. Anna lived in a house directly opposite a Catholic church. He shared a draughty, L-shaped room behind the kitchen with his cousin Eugene, and did most of his schoolwork sitting on the bed. He recalled that from their window, he and Eugene could see the pointed tower of a castle. He went to school nearby, a Russian gymnasium, and every Friday he took a bus home to his village.

We arrived at a small square near the river, just as the sun was setting. My father led us to a low single-storey house opposite a church. Next to the house was a gate opening on to a courtyard, where an elderly woman was watering tomato plants. Alex spoke to her in Ukrainian, and I gathered that she didn't know anything about a Mrs Treichman or any of the house's previous owners. But she invited us to look around. My wife took my hand.

Alex held open a wooden door at the side of the house and the three of us stepped inside. We were standing in an L-shaped room, not much bigger than a pantry – a cold, damp storage area behind the kitchen. Standing there, heads bent, we took up most of the available space. For a moment, I felt the loneliness that my father must have felt, sleeping away from his parents. I asked him if he knew what had become of Mrs Treichman. 'Auschwitz,' he said. 'I think she was killed on the day she arrived.' He glanced around the room. 'No, I don't think this is the house.'

I looked around again too – the room was L-shaped and through the little window I saw the castle. I started to speak. My father said, 'Let's go. I want to get back to the hotel.'

He stepped outside, and I followed him.

'Are you OK?' I asked.

'I'm fine, this just isn't the house.'

'Do you think it's the one next door?' I asked him.

'No, it's all right. Let's just go back to the hotel.'

'Are you sure? We can have Alex ask the neighbours.'

'No, no – it's fine. Let's just go.'

Obviously, while planning the trip, I had thought about

how my father might feel returning to the world that he'd left when he was nineteen. When I'd discussed the itinerary with him some months earlier, he'd told me he was thrilled, really looking forward to seeing the places we planned to visit – but I knew this trip wouldn't be easy. I went to put my arm around his shoulder, to say something more, to insist on what I felt we both knew to be true. 'But Dad, you were so certain – you led us straight here.'

He moved away. 'I'll wait at the corner.'

I thanked the woman in English and Alex translated my words. By the time we finished our goodbyes and shut the gate behind us, my father was crossing the square, walking back towards the centre of town. Watching him disappear up a side street, my wife looked at me. 'Is your dad all right?' she asked.

'Why won't he remember?' I replied.

'What do you mean?' she asked.

'This is it, but I think he's convinced himself this can't be it – and he doesn't want to talk about it.'

The next morning, we drove to a small village called Makar'ovo, about eleven miles to the south, where my father was born. As we got close, he pointed out the former houses of cousins, grandparents and great-grandparents, and the empty land where the synagogue once stood. 'There's Ackerman's,' he said, pointing to a boarded-up breeze-block building at a quiet intersection. 'My mother would buy our groceries there.'

My father told Alex to turn right. 'Grandma's house is just up here,' he said to me. We passed several houses and then he told Alex to stop. We were in front of a low-roofed, squat house where, my father told us, he'd lived with his parents, brothers and sister. Alex left us in the car while he went to speak to some people standing by the side of the road. An elderly couple came out of the house where my father was born. Alex spoke to them for a few minutes and then he gestured for us to join him. We were invited to explore the house and we did, but during the half-hour we spent there my father showed no signs of recognising anything about it. Walking back to the car, he turned to me and said, 'No, I think it must be another house.'

'Let's walk up the road and look at the other houses,' I said.

'No, it's all right, let's just keep going.' My wife came up and I told her that my dad wasn't certain this was my grand-mother's house.

'I just don't think this is it,' he said to her.

'Let's ask the neighbours, someone may know something,' she said, 'I'll get Alex.'

'No, I'd rather not. I'd like to go,' he said.

'Dad, we've come such a long way, we don't have to get in the car just yet,' I said.

'No, no – it's fine. Let's just go.'

We then drove the nine miles to Nehrovo – which is hardly

a village, more a group of three or four farms – to see the farm that had once belonged to my great-grandfather. Many years ago, my mother told me that my father had been left with his grandparents when he was three, so that his mother could care for his younger siblings. Sharing a bedroom with his austere, religious grandfather, he'd lived with these grandparents, on and off, for most of his childhood. Alex spoke to a woman who now lived there, and she gave us permission to walk around. My father pointed out the old house, the farm buildings and the stables. Looking at the farm from the top of a hill, my father told us that there'd once been a mill on the property. Alex said, 'Oh it's still there, by the road, straight ahead.'

'No, no, the mill was much bigger,' my father said. 'That can't be it.'

We all walked up to the building and through a dusty window saw the round millstone. It seemed obvious to everyone but my father that this was the mill and that little had changed in a hundred years. I said, 'Dad, I think it's just that things that seemed big to us as kids look smaller when we see them again as adults – I'm sure it's the same mill.'

'It's getting late,' my father said. 'I think we should be getting back.'

We all got into the car. On the drive back to the hotel, no one spoke – Alex asked if we minded him turning on the radio.

We were supposed to spend the next morning at a resort

in the Carpathians that his family used to visit each summer, but I began to wonder, what was the point? We were ticking off each of the places on our itinerary, and yet the conversations I'd hoped to have with my father weren't taking place.

Over a beer that night, I apologised to Alex for my father's lack of appreciation for the work he'd done. Alex listened, nodding his head as I spoke, and then he told me about another client of his, a woman from Buenos Aires. Her village was made up of a few dozen houses on the Polish–Russian border. 'First the Nazis destroyed it,' Alex told me. 'Then whatever was left, the Soviets took. Even the cobblestones from the old roads are gone.'

The woman had contacted Alex and together they'd returned to her home. 'The only thing that's left of her village is a big oak tree that was in the village square,' he said. The next year, the woman returned with her sister, and in the following years with a friend, then with her children, then with her grandchildren. Every year Alex and his client walked half a mile across a muddy field to where the village had been and, starting from the tree, paced out its streets and houses. '"This was where my grandmother's house was," she says, "the synagogue was here, my home was here."' Alex put down his glass. 'There's nothing there, and she sees everything. With your father, everything is here, and he sees nothing.'

He looked at me. 'Everyone does this differently,' he said.

At the airport, my father saw me hand Alex an envelope.

'You tipped him?' my father asked, shaking his head. 'Crazy! Why would you give him any more money?'

I felt the anger of the previous days rise in me again. 'He found everything, Dad,' I told him. 'He couldn't have done more for us.'

Later, when I was back in London, and back to my psycho-analytic work, I had the thought that my father's remembering and un-remembering may have expressed a simple psycho-logical truth: namely that, emptied of the people he loved, the places we visited were no longer the places he'd known. But more than that, I came to feel increasingly uneasy about my birthday gift to my father. I'd often discussed with my patients the fact that a gift could be controlling, even cruel – is that what I was doing? I'd invited him on the trip, what did I want from him?

The trip had made me aware, too, that the Holocaust had deprived my father of the opportunity of thinking about his childhood. He was sent away from home, first to his grandparents' farm and then to school. And I saw, in a way that I never had before, that he must have felt neglected, that the Holocaust had eclipsed his own early hardship. Having escaped annihilation, he could only say of his upbringing, 'I was lucky.'

Then, almost a year after our journey, I came across a newspaper article about horseback treks in Scotland. I cut out the article to send to my sister, suggesting that she might be interested. She had loved riding as a girl. My father used to take her riding every weekend at a nearby stable. Somewhere there's a photograph that my mother took of the two of them: my sister is twelve years old, smiling as she watches my father bridle a horse. I remembered asking my father once how he knew so much about horses. He started to tell me that he'd spent a lot of time around horses as a boy, at his grandfather's farm. When I asked him if he'd ever had a horse of his own, he abruptly changed the subject and walked away – much like the way he'd walked away from me on the first night of our stay in Mukachevo.

Naturally, these recollections led me to think again about how I've chosen to spend my days: alone with another person, thinking – trying to be present. More often than not, my patients are committed to working together for as long as it takes.

Sometimes, like Alex, I take my patients back to the place they started from, using whatever landmarks remain. I too help them pace out an invisible but palpable world. At times, I feel I'm a tour guide – part detective, part translator. And he's right – everyone does this differently.

But this wasn't quite the whole story. Eight months after our trip, my daughter, Clara, was born. One day, when Clara was five years old, she overheard me talking on the telephone. My father had called to tell me that a cousin of ours, a woman I'd known all my life, had died.

My cousin, Toby, was born Teresa Grosz. Her grandfather and my father's grandfather were brothers. She was born and raised on the farm at Nehrovo. When my father emigrated to America in 1940, Toby and her family remained. In April 1944 everyone living on the farm was taken by the Nazis, first to the brick factory in Mukachevo, where they were kept for several days without food or water, then, in cattle cars, to Auschwitz. On arrival, Toby, her sister Helen, and Eugene, my father's school room-mate – all teenagers at the time – had their heads shaved and their arms tattooed with a number. They were put to work. The rest of my father's family, and almost everyone else my father knew, were sent to the gas chambers.

On the phone, my father and I talked about Toby's life. He and Toby had played together on the farm; he remembered that she had been a happy girl. But she had never really adjusted to life in America, he said. 'She lived here more than sixty years, but this was never home.'

I hung up the phone, and my daughter appeared in the doorway. She asked me about what she'd heard. In response to my daughter's questions – about Auschwitz, and about the Nazis – I found myself struggling to find the right words. I saw in myself, and now recognised in my father, the impulse to keep such horror from my children.

On bearing death

My patient, Lucy N., a young research scientist, put her coat
and scarf on the couch and sat down in the chair opposite me.
'I don't want to lie down today, I don't want therapy.'

She looked at me directly. 'Don't worry,' she said. 'I haven't
stopped eating. I had dinner last night and some breakfast
this morning. I just want to tell you what's happened.'

This session was at 9 a.m. on a Friday morning. Just after
midnight the night before, Lucy had gone to sleep on the sofa
in the living room of her parents' house. Her mother dozed
on the other sofa. A nurse was with her father in her parents'
bedroom. A few hours later, at about 4.30, she'd felt her mother
leaning over her. She put a hand on Lucy's pillow and whis-
pered, 'We need to go into the bedroom now.'

In the bedroom, the nurse had all the lights on. Her mother
sat down in a chair. Lucy walked around to the other side of
the bed and sat down next to her father. His head was tilted

back, his mouth wide open, his breathing very shallow. Lucy touched his forehead and his cheek, and then she took his hand.

When her father let out a strange gasp, her mother made a noise. 'It sounded like "Eugh",' Lucy said. 'Maybe she was surprised, not disgusted, but it annoyed me. Even the way she was holding his hand annoyed me. She wasn't *holding* it. She kept patting it lightly, with her fingertips, saying "There, there – there, there." I wanted to tell her to stop, but I didn't. I just tried to stay focused on my father.

'Then the nurse said, "He's going." So I lay down on the bed next to him. I put my head next to his on the pillow. I put my hand on his chest and leaned my forehead against the side of his face. His beard was rough and it reminded me of when I was little and he used to kiss me good morning. I was remembering this when I felt my mother's hand on my shoulder, shaking me, telling me to get up. I didn't want to, but I did – straight away. I didn't want to show her up in front of the nurse.

'As I sat up he opened his eyes for a brief moment. He looked straight ahead at the ceiling. I don't think he could see anything. And then he closed his eyes and he was gone.'

The nurse left the room and her mother followed her out. A few seconds later, her mother poked her head around the door and told Lucy that she needed her. 'She wanted to talk to me about what to do next. I told her that I needed just a few minutes alone with Dad.'

The sun was starting to come up. Lucy opened the curtains and turned off the lights. She wanted the room to be the way her father liked it. She sat down on the bed. 'And then I just talked to him,' she said.

She told him she was relieved that he wasn't in pain any more, that he was at peace. 'I told him I loved him and I said I was sorry for any pain I might have caused him. I told him that he would always be with me. And I kissed him.'

It had been only a few minutes, she said, but his lips felt cool. She sat there silently with him.

After a while, she went into the kitchen, made a pot of tea and telephoned her brother and uncles. And when she'd finished those calls, she went outside – so her mother wouldn't overhear – and phoned me to say that her father had died, and to ask if I had an extra hour to meet this morning. Then she sat in the kitchen. She felt tired, but she had no desire to sleep.

During the past few days, while her father was dying, she'd often felt on the verge of exploding at her mother; she could feel the resentment building within her. 'I'm afraid I'm going to snap at her. She was crap at looking after me, and she was crap at looking after my dad, but it won't do much good to tell her that now.'

Lucy looked at her watch. 'I know it's time to stop, but can I tell you one more thing?'

'Of course,' I said. 'What is it?'

'I had a dream. I'm worried I'll forget it. I think I was having it when my mum woke me.'

In the dream, Lucy was travelling on a train with a newborn baby. She knew it wasn't her baby – how could it be? But there was no one else to look after him, and he was hungry, so she put the baby to her breast and found she had milk. He was soothed and fell asleep. It was then that she realised that the baby was her father. She didn't know how she knew it was him, but it definitely was. This wasn't upsetting, just a fact.

'I don't have a clue what it's about,' Lucy said. 'It's so strange about the baby.'

'Strange in what way?' I asked.

'I've never dreamed about a baby like this before. This dream felt – different.'

The undertaker was coming at 10.30 and Lucy still had to go back to her own flat for some fresh clothes. 'Maybe we can talk about the dream next week,' she said.

But we didn't talk about the dream the following week. She was overtaken by events – organising her father's funeral, choosing someone to write his obituary, and coping with her mother's behaviour after the service. The week after that, there was the matter of her dad's will. Lucy used her sessions to try and settle these problems, to consider her father's life and the months leading up to his death – was there anything more she could've done? – and to imagine the years ahead without him.

My first intuitions about the dream had to do with the reasons Lucy had come to see me in the first place. Lucy had been referred to me two years earlier, when she was twenty-seven, because she'd had a violent resurgence of her adolescent anorexia. When she was sixteen, she'd been hospitalised and had almost died. At our first meeting, she looked like a waif, malnourished, watery and limp. Her weight was down, and her periods had stopped altogether. Her hair was dull and her skin pallid. Although she had a boyfriend and a cat, her only interest seemed to be her postdoctoral research project. But even in this area, she was struggling with self-doubt. 'I should've stopped at an MSc. Then I'd be working for someone else, carrying out their experiments, not having to devise research ideas of my own. I'm incapable of generating any original ideas.'

The picture she had of the interior of her body was just as barren. More often than not, she felt herself incapable of feeding or caring for herself. The idea of having a baby just didn't even figure.

But during the last three months of her father's life, as she cared for him, her own health seemed to improve, perhaps because she was cooking for and feeding him. Having to care for his body was making her more thoughtful about her own. Nevertheless, her dream of nursing an infant to sleep felt faintly menacing to me. For many years, Lucy had struggled with her parents. During our sessions, if she wasn't attacking herself, she was attacking them. At times, she behaved as if she had to kill her parents to become herself. My first thought was that the dream probably arose from her unconscious feeling that there was something deadly in her that – could she but feed it to her father – would help him to die. But it turned out that I was completely wrong.

Four months after she'd first described the dream to me, Lucy walked into my consulting room and told me that she was pregnant. She sat on the couch and told me about buying the testing kit, peeing on the stick, and watching, in disbelief, as the blue line appeared. She was deeply happy.

She and her boyfriend didn't use birth control because she was convinced she couldn't get pregnant, not with her irregular periods. How could this have happened? she wondered, laughing. 'Obviously I know that the male gamete and the female gamete fused to produce a zygote. But I'm wondering about how *I* came to be able to be pregnant. Perhaps it was the dream,' she said.

'*A* dream?' I asked.

'*The* dream. The dream I had the night my father died.'

We talked again about her father's final days. He'd been unable to speak, and she'd had to change his incontinence pants regularly. On some nights, because he was frightened, she'd sat with him until the sun came up. And although we hadn't yet talked about the dream, Lucy claimed to know what I'd made of it.

'What did I think?' I asked.

'That by looking after my dad, I'd learned that I was capable of looking after a baby. You didn't say it, but I expected you to say, "Your mum isn't in the dream. The dream is about *you* being a mother. You can be a mother, because you've discovered you don't have to be a mother like your mum." I thought the train we were riding on might represent a new train of thought. The dream was really pretty straightforward.'

Lucy was quiet for a moment, and then she described a colleague at work who'd been unable to conceive, even with IVF. After being approved by an adoption agency, she got pregnant. 'She needed someone to tell her she'd be a good mother. My dream was like that, I was giving myself approval to get pregnant, don't you think?'

'I hadn't seen it like that at the time,' I said, 'but I think you're right.' It seemed to me too that Lucy had found her voice – a way of putting her own feelings into her own words – not just with me, but also in spite of me.

For the rest of the session, she talked about the plans she and her boyfriend were making: they would turn the study into a nursery; eventually, when he got a pay rise, they'd be able to afford a bigger place.

As I listened to Lucy, I imagined her with a newborn baby.

I saw her sitting in the park with her baby, and then, some years later, walking her child to school. I felt that she was right, she was changed – and that the end of our work had begun.

Leaving

Through silence

Anthony M. had been seeing me for three months when, after much discussion, he went to get tested for HIV. Several days later, he sat on the couch and sobbed into his hands – at age twenty-nine, he had just been told that he was HIV-positive. It was 1989, and there was no treatment for AIDS.

His doctor in London wouldn't tell him how much longer he could expect to live, so he asked an old friend, a physician in San Francisco. With his immune system, his friend told him, he could 'expect to live for two years and hope to live four'.

In the weeks immediately following his test results he reported many dreams – of aeroplanes falling out of the sky, tornados churning up the earth. He had one dream in which everyone had AIDS. We understood this to mean that if everyone had AIDS, then no one had AIDS. Anthony felt isolated, frightened and alone.

During this time, Anthony continued to speak about his life and his feelings, but his flow of words became slower and slower, until one day he became altogether silent. Sometimes he would come in, speak with me about work or family, a relationship or a doctor's appointment, and then go quiet. On other days, he might lie down and be silent for the entire fifty minutes. 'I just feel so sad,' he told me, at the end of one such session.

It is difficult for me to convey the feeling of these sessions – the overwhelming stillness and heaviness in the consulting room. There was nothing numbing about the silences; if anything, I listened more attentively. I sat forward, on the edge of my chair. There are silences that are anxious, where the patient – arms folded, eyes open – refuses to speak. There are uncomfortable silences, following a disclosure of something intimate or sexual, say. Anthony's silences were wholly different; he wasn't resisting or self-conscious. Under ordinary circumstances, I might ask a patient who has been silent for some time what they're thinking or feeling, and once or twice I did this with Anthony. But I soon realised that my speaking was an intrusion, a disturbance.

As I sat with him, day after day, Anthony's silences grew deeper and deeper. One day, lying very still, his breathing slow and regular, he fell into a deep sleep. The first time this happened, he woke up a little embarrassed. 'I think I'm just very tired,' he said. 'How long was I asleep?' But soon, he was regularly sleeping ten or fifteen minutes in most sessions, and usually one full session once or twice a week. He told me that it didn't feel like sleep – it was more like passing out, being given a general anaesthetic. He was never sure how long he'd been asleep.

My first thought was that he was sleeping in his sessions because he was too anxious to sleep through the night at home. He felt safe with me; I would watch over him while he slept.

Sometimes he'd dream while on the couch. On one occasion, about nine months into his analysis, Anthony was lying on his side. He looked across the room at my bookcase, closed his eyes, and went to sleep.

When he woke up twenty minutes later, he told me that he'd dreamed he was looking in a medical textbook. In the book, there was a cutaway photograph of a foetus inside its mother. Even though it was in a book, the image was moving. He watched blood passing between the mother and the baby via the umbilical cord. The caption under the image read 'This baby is being infected by the mother's blood, because the mother is HIV-positive.' A wind came up, turning the book's pages, 'like in the movies when the wind blows the pages of a calendar'. And then he woke up.

Based on what I knew about Anthony, and my ideas about the transference – how we all construct each other according to early blueprints – I took this dream as an expression of his desire to be close to me but also to keep me at a distance. He wanted to feel contained by me, but he was afraid that I was poisonous. We worked out that he was frightened that my words might harm him, make him ill, like the foetus who was being infected by the mother. He said, 'I get scared that if we talk about it, or even if we think about it, I'll get ill.'

I thought I understood what was happening in the analysis and wrote it up as a lecture. But shortly after my lecture was published in the *International Journal of Psychoanalysis*, I began to feel uneasy about what I'd written. Anthony would still fall asleep during his sessions and, as far as I could see, the interpretations I was making were having little effect. I found myself feeling more and more lost in his silences.

After sitting with patients for thousands and thousands of hours, I'd developed an internal clock for fifty minutes. But with Anthony my clock broke. Now, a whole session could go by in what felt like minutes, or just the opposite. On one occasion, as I was about to tell Anthony we'd have to stop, I looked at my watch and discovered only a few minutes had passed. Though I didn't say it to him then, I had the thought that he wanted to stop time – to stay forever in the present, where he was not ill or dying.

Three years into Anthony's psychoanalysis, his immune system collapsed. His CD4 cell count hadn't been in the normal range (500 to 1,500 cells per cubic millimetre of blood) for some time, but suddenly it dropped from 175 to 43. When an individual infected with HIV had a CD4 count of less than 200, he was diagnosed as having AIDS. Although Anthony looked well and was not ill, it was becoming more and more likely that he would soon contract pneumocystis pneumonia or some other potentially fatal infection.

A few days after hearing that Anthony's CD4s were critically low, I received a letter inviting me abroad to a clinical seminar, and I decided to present Anthony's case. I wanted to do so because I had the impression that the work we were doing was unusual, that, more often than not, HIV-positive patients were offered counselling that emphasised advice and reassurance – Anthony called it 'sugar coating'. He told me that he found realism, no matter how painful, was almost always more reassuring than reassurance. In any case, I was convinced that psychoanalysts would be seeing more and more of these patients. During a coffee break, an eminent American psychoanalyst came up to me and said, 'A few of us were talking after your presentation, and I wanted to ask you, why are you wasting your time on this patient? He's going to die. Why not help someone who's got a future?'

His question shocked and angered me. It felt cruel. It seemed clear to Anthony and me that his analysis had helped him to overcome his anxiety and depression, so that he was better able to make use of his physicians. Analysis also helped him to live with the unknown. In his words, 'Live well while you can, die well when you have to.'

Still, the American analyst's question stayed in my mind and made me realise how protective I'd become of my patient.

A few weeks later, Anthony asked me whether I would continue to see him when he was eventually admitted to hospital. I told him that I would come each day for his session; we'd continue seeing each other as we were now, five times a week.

'What if the hospital won't let you?'

'I don't think anyone can stop me coming to see you during visiting hours, pulling up a chair behind you, and us continuing to talk.'

'Maybe they'd let us have a room, but if not we could just draw the curtain around us, couldn't we?'

'You want to know that I will be with you as long as you need me, and I will.'

He replied that he knew I would be with him, and then he cried.

It was after this exchange that we were better able to put into words what he wanted. He would rather commit suicide towards the end, he told me, than feel that the HIV had won. He didn't want to die frightened or alone; as much as possible, he wanted to avoid pain. He didn't want to die in a state of panic or persecution, but to be 'able to live my death'.

Anthony considers himself lucky. Twenty-two years since we first met, his viral load is undetectable and his CD4 count is within the normal range. He's in good health. Because he no longer fears that his illness will become a reality if he thinks or talks about it, he has become proactive in his medical care. And the right drugs came at the right time. 'Take that, you fucker,' he thinks, as he takes his daily dose of pills.

We still meet, but less frequently. And though rare, there are still occasions when he'll fall asleep for a few minutes in a session – usually on the day of a blood test or its result, or after hearing news of the death of a relative or friend. When it happens now, it's a marker, reminding us both that death is nearer than we'd like to believe.

I now think that Anthony's silences expressed different things at different times: sorrow, a desire to be close to me but stay separate, and a wish to stop time. Anthony has told me that he felt these silences were healing too, a chance for him to regress, to be looked after. The deepening quiet was a sign of Anthony's deepening trust. It may be that his silences were also a way of rehearsing the moment of his death, but most of all, they were something we went through together. And in doing so, Anthony found that he could more easily bear the idea of his death, accept the silence, because he felt himself alive in the mind of another.

On closure

My records show that I saw Alice P. for a consultation in June 1988. She began our meeting by telling me, 'I haven't felt myself for years. I don't know how to pull myself out of it.' She told me a little bit about her family. She and her husband wanted to give their two daughters a good start, and 'the girls' had done well – this year, their younger daughter would get her degree in medicine from Oxford. Towards the end of the consultation, Alice sat forward in her chair. She told me that nineteen years earlier, their third child, Jack, had died unexpectedly. He was three months old. 'It was a Friday – the 27th of June, 1969 – just after lunch. I fed Jack and put him down for his nap. When I came back he was dead.'

I listened as Alice then described a passage from C. S. Lewis' *A Grief Observed*, in which Lewis fears that, bit by bit, he is losing the memory of his dead wife: 'like snowflakes settling down on his memory of her until her real shape is hidden, is how Lewis puts it. It's not like that for me,' Alice said, 'I remember everything about Jack – the smell of his skin, his smile, everything.'

Keeping absolutely still she said, 'A couple of days ago I was in the kitchen making breakfast, listening to the radio, and there was that dreadful news story about those kids that got killed in a boating accident. I thought – "Jack's safe from drowning." I think like that: Jack's safe from drunk drivers. Jack won't ever get cancer or have a heart attack – my baby's safe. That's crazy. I shouldn't be thinking like that.'

Six months ago, Edmund K. asked to see me for a consultation. At twenty-nine, Edmund was already the director of an international humanitarian aid organisation. During the previous five years, he had visited over thirty countries, supervising relief work in Afghanistan, Sudan and Iraq. He had been on antidepressants since the age of nineteen, when his father committed suicide. 'I shouldn't have to be on antidepressants,' he said to me. 'But every time I start to come off them, I find myself back where I was when I was nineteen – angry with my dad for killing himself. It's so stupid. I should've had closure on this thing years ago.'

Alice P. and Edmund K. are grieving, each in their own way. What they have in common is this: they suffer more because they're stuck on the idea of closure.

They suffer more because they both expect to make progress, to move through certain stages of grief. And when they don't, they feel that they are doing something wrong, or, more precisely, that there is something wrong with them. They suffer twice – first from grief and then from a tyranny of shoulds: 'I should have pulled myself out of this,' 'I shouldn't be so angry,' 'I should have moved on by now,' and so forth. There is little room here for emotional exploration or under-standing. This way of being leads to self-loathing, despair, depression.

The notion of closure – of having finished with grief – almost certainly has its roots in the work of Elisabeth Kübler-Ross. In the 1960s Kübler-Ross identified five psychological stages in the experience of terminally ill patients, the last of which is acceptance. About twenty-five years ago, Kübler-Ross and many bereavement counsellors began to use these same five stages to describe the experiences of both the dying *and* the grieving.

I've long thought that Kübler-Ross was wrong. The 'psychological stages' of dying and grieving are wholly different. For the person who dies there is an end, but this is not so for the person who grieves. The person who mourns goes on living and for as long as he lives there is always the possibility of feeling grief.

Each of us mourns differently, but in general the initial shock and fear triggered by a death does diminish with time. Through the work of mourning, we gradually feel better, though some heartache remains. Holidays and anniversaries are notoriously difficult. Grief can ebb and then, without warning, resurge. The loss of a child, a loss through suicide – these losses, and many others, can and do cause enduring sorrow.

Nonetheless, closure is what the counselling trade tends to promise. 'Grief Lit' – a burgeoning sub-genre of 'Recovery Lit' – offers these recent titles: *In the Presence of Grief: Helping Family Members Resolve Death, Dying, and Bereavement Issues*; *Grief Steps: Steps to Regroup, Rebuild and Renew After Any Life Loss*; and *The Grief Recovery Handbook*. This last book is Amazon-recommended: 'As a grief facilitator, this is my one and only text for my participants. It is wonderful!' reads one comment, and, 'Add this book to your grief toolbox!' You get the picture: your grief is something that can be fixed. You can recover. You can have closure.

My experience is that closure is an extraordinarily compelling fantasy of mourning. It is the fiction that we can love, lose, suffer and then *do something* to permanently end our sorrow. We want to believe we can reach closure because grief can surprise and disorder us – even years after our loss.

On Friday 15 November 2008, a brush fire swept through the hills and canyons above Montecito, California, injuring more than two dozen people and destroying 210 homes. One of those homes belonged to my sister. Though unhurt, she and her husband lost everything but the clothes they were wearing.

A month after the fire, when we were speaking on the phone, my sister told me about the way that the community had pulled together – restaurants were donating free meals to those who'd lost something in the fire. She described the process of getting federal aid, the various loans available, and told me how helpful a government employee had been with her application.

I told my sister that I admired her pragmatism, her ability to pick herself up and get on with things.

Then she told me that she'd been to see a clairvoyant.

I was surprised by this, but still more by my own reaction. When my sister told me that she'd talked to our mother – who has been dead for more than twenty years – I became tearful and heard myself ask her, 'What did Mom say?'

After we had finished our phone call I had the thought that we turn to clairvoyance when we need our dead and can't accept death's finality. We want to believe that the clairvoyant can bring our dead back into the world of the living. Closure is just as delusive – it is the false hope that we can deaden our living grief.

On waking from a dream

A couple of years ago, just before Christmas, my four-year-old son was admitted to hospital. He'd developed an infection called preseptal cellulitis in the skin around his right eye – his eyelid was angry-red and swollen shut. Doctors worried the infection could travel into the optic nerve and then into his brain. He was given intravenous penicillin and monitored around the clock. For seven days, my wife and I stayed with him, and fell into step with life on the children's ward – our son's regular doses of medicine, the nurses' twelve-hour shifts, the doctors' morning rounds. The snow-muffled streets increased our sense of isolation.

On his first night back home, my son refused to take his antibiotics. My wife and I were alternately pleading, tearful and angry, all to no avail. Finally, I told him a story about the time I had to have my tonsils out, and had run away from two nurses when they came to take me to the operating theatre.

'I just didn't want to go,' I said. My son considered this, and, after a few minutes, agreed to take his medicine. At bedtime, with the stories read and the lights turned off, he asked me to tell him again about the time I ran away from the nurses.

That night I was startled awake by a dream, which began to dissolve as soon as I woke. I had an image of myself reaching out to catch a small grass-green lizard that had shot down a dark space between two rocks, vanishing into the earth. The dream felt like a memory – it had the colours of an old photograph, perhaps something that had actually happened to me when I was a boy. I thought the dream might have something to do with my son's illness, but what? Then I remembered another detail from the dream, the four letters S, I, D, A.

I lay in the dark for a few moments running after the dream but failing to remember any more. Frustrated, I got out of bed, went to the kitchen and ran myself a glass of water from the tap. The green digital clock on the oven said 01.25. I took my glass and went to the living room at the top of the house. I sat there in the quiet, the hush interrupted only occasionally by an all-night bus changing gears on the hill around the corner.

As a psychoanalyst, I feel uncomfortable when I can't remember a dream. It's irrational of course, but failing to remember a dream makes me feel a bit embarrassed, a bit of a fraud. 'You can dish it out, but you can't take it,' I've thought to myself on more than one occasion. That night, I did what psychoanalysts tell their patients to do when trying to recapture the details of a dream: I let my mind free associate – allowing any thought I had float to the surface, no matter how illogical or embarrassing.

My first thought: a Spanish poem. Was it by Pedro Salinas? I knew it wasn't exact, but I remembered: 'I forgot your name; the letters of your name move about now unconnected, unknown to each other / Rearranged they form advertisements on buses, they're on envelopes shaping other names / You're somewhere now, but all in bits, dismantled, impossible.'

In a rush, I recognised the four letters: SIDA is Spanish for AIDS, but also the very same letters rearranged – like the letters in the poem, moved about.

I remembered a young man who had come to see me years ago for two consultations. He'd been referred by his family doctor because he was HIV-positive and refusing treatment for pneumonia. Could I find some way of encouraging him to listen to his doctor or parents?

During our first meeting the young man told me that he was born and raised in Cornwall, in a small village at the tip of the Lizard. 'The Lizard is a peninsula, the southernmost point in Britain, in fact – the Spanish Armada was first sighted from the field next to my parent's house,' he said. We talked about his illness, but his lack of concern for himself disturbed me. I did my best to reach him. We discussed his fear of dying, and I suggested that his defence against this anxiety was to deny that he was ill and to refuse treatment. He left unconvinced of the need for help, but promised to return for a second meeting the next day.

He was late for our appointment. When he arrived, he told me that he'd realised I was right, that he needed to look after himself. But instead of accepting treatment, he'd decided that the best thing to do was to take a break. He'd already booked a trip to Rio for Mardi Gras – why not go earlier?

The following autumn I heard from his doctor that he had died – not from pneumonia, but from dysentery.

Outside, another night bus went by. These two consultations, which did not seem that long ago, must have taken place at least twenty years earlier. The young man was only twenty-six years old when he died. His parents were probably still alive. I imagined their home by the sea and the field next to it blanketed with snow. I saw them as they might be now, wrapping gifts, listening to the radio, remembering their beautiful boy in his flannel pyjamas, opening his presents on Christmas morning.

I wish I could have somehow persuaded him to take his medicine, to come into hospital, to let his physicians treat him. But he was, like the lizard in my dream, out of reach.

I did not know the words then, and I probably could not find the words now that would persuade him to stay. Looking up, I became aware of my reflection in the large dark window. I again felt my helplessness of the previous evening – my momentary powerlessness at my son's refusal to take his medicine, and my fear that he too could disappear into the earth.

Now, so many of the patients I saw when I was young are gone or dead, but sometimes, as when waking from a dream, I find myself reaching out to them, wanting to say one more thing.

Sources and Notes

Preface

I have taken care to protect patients' confidentiality. I have changed names and altered any identifying particulars so as to preserve my patients' anonymity without distorting the nature of our work together. If I was uncertain, I showed my patient the draft and invited comment: all were willing to share their experience; many expressed the hope that their story would help others.

Simone Weil, *Gravity and Grace* (London: Routledge and Kegan Paul, 1952) p. 132.

Beginnings

HOW WE CAN BE POSSESSED BY A STORY THAT CANNOT BE TOLD

The quotation from Karen Blixen (Isak Dinesen), 'All sorrows can be borne if you put them into a story or tell a story about them,' is an epigraph to the chapter on action in Hannah Arendt's *The Human Condition* (Chicago: University of Chicago Press; 2nd revised edition, 1999).

D. W. Winnicott, 'The Concept of Trauma in Relation to the Development of the Individual within the Family' in *Psycho-Analytic Explorations*, Clare Winnicott, Ray Shepherd and Madeleine Davis (eds.) (London: Karnac Books, 1989).

ON LAUGHTER

Joseph Sandler, 'Countertransference and Role-Responsiveness', *International Review of Psycho-Analysis*, 1976, 3:43–47.

HOW PRAISE CAN CAUSE A LOSS OF CONFIDENCE

Carol S. Dweck and Claudia M. Mueller, 'Praise for Intelligence Can Undermine Children's Motivation and Performance', *Journal of Personality and Social Psychology*, 1998, Vol. 75, No. 1, 33–52.

Anne Enright, *Making Babies: Stumbling into Motherhood* (London: Vintage, 2005).

THE GIFT OF PAIN

Phillip Yancey and Paul Brand, *The Gift of Pain: Why We Hurt and What We Can Do About It* (Grand Rapids, Michigan: Zondervan Publishing, 1997).

Joyce McDougall, 'Reflections on Affect: A Psychoanalytic View on Alexithymia' in *Theatres of the Mind: Illusion and Truth on the Psychoanalytic Stage* (London: Free Association Books, 1986).

Loving

HOW PARANOIA CAN RELIEVE SUFFERING AND PREVENT A CATASTROPHE

E. L. Auchincloss, R. W. Weiss, 'Paranoid Character and the Intolerance of Indifference', *Journal of the American Psychoanalytic Association*, 1992, 40:1013–37.

Paul Fussell, *The Great War and Modern Memory*, (Oxford: Oxford University Press, 2000).

WHY PARENTS ENVY THEIR CHILDREN
Betty Joseph, 'Envy in Everyday Life', in *Psychic Equilibrium and Psychic Change* (London: Tavistock Routledge, 1989).

ON HATE
Sigmund Freud (1912), 'On the Universal Tendency to Debasement in the Sphere of Love (Contributions to the Psychology of Love II)' in *The Standard Edition of the Complete Psychological Works of Sigmund Freud, Volume XI* (London: The Hogarth Press and the Institute of Psychoanalysis, 1978).

HOW LOVESICKNESS KEEPS US FROM LOVE
Charles Dickens, 'A Christmas Carol' in *A Christmas Carol and Other Christmas Books* (Oxford: Oxford University Press, 2008), pp. 5–85.

Changing

HOW A FEAR OF LOSS CAN CAUSE US TO LOSE EVERYTHING
Jim Dwyer and Kevin Flynn, *102 Minutes: The Untold Story of the Fight to Survive inside the Twin Towers* (London: Arrow, 2005).

Leonard Shengold, *Haunted by Parents* (New Haven, Connecticut: Yale University Press, 2006).

Alix Spiegel, *Analysis: Studies into Psychology During Disasters*, Weekend All Things Considered, National Public Radio, 11 September 2004.

HOW NEGATIVITY PREVENTS OUR SURRENDER TO LOVE

Stuart S. Asch, 'Varieties of Negative Therapeutic Reaction and Problems of Technique', *Journal of the American Psychoanalytic Association*, 1976, 24:383–407.

Anna Freud, 'Notes on a Connection Between the States of Negativism and of Emotional Surrender' in *The Writings of Anna Freud: Indications for Child Analysis and Other Papers 1945–1956* (New York: International Universities Press, 1968).

Dan McCall, *The Silence of Bartleby* (Ithaca, New York: Cornell University Press, 1989).

Herman Melville, 'Bartleby, the Scrivener' in *Billy Budd, Sailor and Other Stories* (London: Everyman, 1993).

ON LOSING A WALLET

Anna Freud, 'About Losing and Being Lost', *The Psychoanalytic Study of the Child*, 1967, 22:9–19.

Karen Horney, 'The Problem of the Negative Therapeutic Reaction', *Psychoanalytic Quarterly*, 1936, 5:29–44.

Dr Seuss, *Did I Ever Tell You How Lucky You Are?* (London: HarperCollins, 2004).

William Styron, *Darkness Visible: A Memoir of Madness* (London: Picador, 1991).

WHY WE LURCH FROM CRISIS TO CRISIS

D. W. Winnicott, 'Psychoanalysis and the Sense of Guilt' in *The Maturational Processes and the Facilitating Environment* (London: The Hogarth Press and the Institute of Psychoanalysis, 1979).

ON BEING BORING

Samuel Beckett, *Endgame* in *The Complete Dramatic Works* (London: Faber and Faber, 1986), p.128.

Betty Joseph, 'The Patient Who Is Difficult To Reach' in *Psychic Equilibrium and Psychic Change* (London: Tavistock / Routledge, 1989).

GOING BACK

See: Arthur Krystal's 'My Holocaust Problem' in *The Half-Life of an American Essayist* (Jaffrey, New Hampshire: David R. Godine, 2007). Krystal's essay addresses many of the issues touched on here, also from a personal perspective. He writes: 'If the life of the mind is a series of steps involving the progressive loss of innocence, beginning with the realization that one is not the center of the universe and ending with the thought that the universe itself has no center, surely there is no need to accelerate a child's journey toward the programmed horror that the German leaders conceived for the Jews. People will come to such knowledge on their own, or they won't. I am not sure that the examined life requires the contemplation of what happened to the Jews. All I am sure of is that because those who perished had no choice in their deaths, we, their descendants, have no choice but to remember.'

Leaving

THROUGH SILENCE

Stephen Grosz, 'A Phantasy of Infection', *International Journal of Psychoanalysis*, 1993, 74:965–74.

ON WAKING FROM A DREAM

Pedro Salinas, 'Muertes / Deaths' in *Roots and Wings: Poetry from Spain, 1900–1975: A Bilingual Anthology*, Hardie St. Martin (ed.) (London: Harper and Row, 1976). Poem translated by W. S. Merwin.

Acknowledgements

Loving thanks to my wife, Nicola, who generously gave her time and understanding. This book is dedicated to her and the two other people who made it possible, our children, Clara and Samuel.

Carin Besser, Wendy Cope, David Aaronovitch and John Lahr have read and reread these stories for as long as I have been writing them. Without their advice, I could not have written this book.

Thanks to the friends and family who have provided encouragement and help, among them, Christopher Bollas, Michael Brearley, Donald Campbell, Ann Y. Coxon, Alex Dunai, my parents Anita and Bernard, my brother Mick and sister Jacalyn, Frances Kolman Gross, Jack Gross, David Harrison, Sarah Jones, Julia Kreitman, Stephen Lehmann and Carol Sabersky, Geoffrey and Janice Luckhurst, Lachlan Mackinnon, Paul Mayersberg, Michael Mitchell, Alan

Montefiore and Catherine Audard, Penny Pilzer, Celia Read, John Scholar, Michael and Angela Scholar, Jonathan Sheldon, Stuart Sherman, Clive Sinclair, Ramaswamy Sudarshan, Katharine Viner and Bettina von Zwehl.

Elizabeth Bradshaw, Molly Macdonald, Siân Putnam and Sharon Shamir helped with the preparation of this book. I thank them all for their suggestions and good humour.

To these psychoanalysts I owe a special debt: Amadeo Limentani, Anne-Marie Sandler, Hanna Segal and Ignês Sodré. I am grateful to them, and to colleagues and students at the Institute of Psychoanalysis, and the Psychoanalysis Unit, University College, London, and also colleagues at the Portman Clinic, the Anna Freud Centre, the Royal Free Hospital and Gloucester House at the Tavistock Clinic.

David Miller has been the most encouraging and thoughtful agent. I thank him, and his colleagues at Rogers, Coleridge & White – especially Stephen Edwards, Alex Goodwin, Margaret Halton, Laurence Laluyaux, Zoë Nelson, Peter Robinson, Eleanor Simpson and Peter Straus. My thanks also to Melanie Jackson in New York.

I am deeply indebted to my publisher and editor at Chatto & Windus, Clara Farmer. I thank her and Parisa Ebrahimi for the care and imagination they have shown during the editing and publishing of this book. Thank you to everyone at Chatto for making our work together so pleasurable, especially David Milner, Stephen Parker and Sue Amaradivakara.

Many thanks to the other publishers who have been involved in this project, above all: Maria Guarnaschelli at W.W. Norton in New York, Anne Collins at Random House Canada in Toronto, Martijn David and Erna Staal at Contact Atlas in Holland, Nina Bschorr and Peter Sillem at S. Fischer Verlag in Frankfurt, Francesco Anzelmo at Arnoldo Mondadori Editore in Milan, Miguel Aguilar at Random House Mondadori S.A in Barcelona, Jorge Zahar in Brazil and Anna Pataki of S. Patakis Publications S.A. in Athens.

Parts of this book have appeared in the *Financial Times Weekend Magazine*; my thanks to Caroline Daniel, Alice Fishburn, Sue Matthias and Annabel Wright.

My greatest debt, finally, is to those who cannot be thanked by name – the patients whose lives have shaped this book.